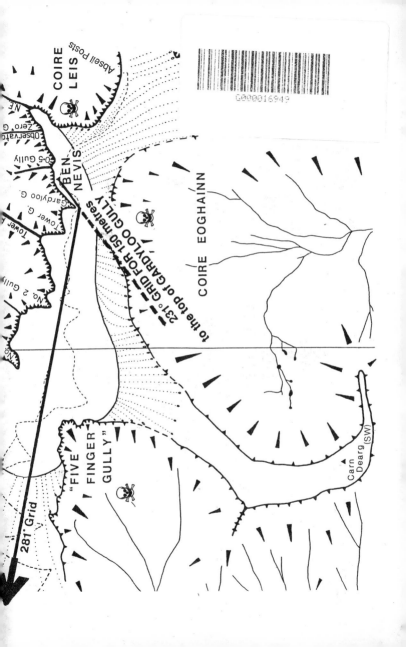

COIRE LEIS

Abseil Posts

COIRE EOGHAINN

BEN NEVIS

NE

Observatory
Zero G.

0·5 Gully

Gardyloo G.

Tower G.

No. 2 Gully

No.

231° GRID FOR 150 metres / GARDYLOO GULLY to the top of

"FIVE FINGER GULLY"

Carn Dearg (SW)

281° Grid

G000016949

WINTER CLIMBS
BEN NEVIS & GLEN COE

Looking across from Zero Gully to climbers entering the 'Basin' on Orion Face Direct

WINTER CLIMBS
BEN NEVIS
& GLEN COE

by

ALAN KIMBER

Diagrams by Kevin Howett
(except where stated)

CICERONE PRESS
MILNTHORPE, CUMBRIA

© Alan Kimber 1994
ISBN 1 85284 179 6

First Edition (by I.S.Clough) March 1969
Second Edition (Revised by H.MacInnes) March 1974
Third Edition (by Ed Grindley) February 1981
Fourth Edition (by Alan Kimber) February 1991
Fifth Edition (by Alan Kimber) October 1994

Advice to Readers

Readers are advised that whilst every effort is taken by the author to ensure the accuracy of this guidebook, changes can occur which may affect the contents. It is advisable to check locally on transport, accommodation, shops etc but even rights-of-way can be altered and, more especially overseas, paths can be eradicated by landslip, forest fires or changes of ownership.

The publisher would welcome notes of any such changes

Front cover: Mega Route X (VI,6), Central Trident Buttress,
                 Ben Nevis. Climber 'Cubby' Cuthbertson

Back cover: Stob Dearg - Buchaille Etive Mor, Glen Coe

CONTENTS

PREFACE & ACKNOWLEDGEMENTS

This new edition of *Winter Climbs - Ben Nevis and Glen Coe*, has many new routes, some new areas, more information and up-dated illustrations. The Ben Nevis and Aonach Mor/Beag area is 99% complete and Glen Coe has a 70% coverage. All of the most popular areas have been described.

Whilst compiling the details I have had considerable help from a wide range of climbers who have been kind enough to give time and thought to my questions. Particular thanks are due to Kev Howett for supplying some excellent new diagrams which I believe have added a touch of class and make the book much easier to use. My thanks go to the following people: Jim Blyth; Robin Clothier; Ken Crocket; Dave 'Cubby' Cuthbertson; Mal Duff; Con Higgins; Paul Moores; Arthur Paul; Godefroy Perroux; Simon Richardson; and the SMC for allowing considerable use to be made of their 'Journal' and guidebooks; Noel Williams; Roger Wild; Blyth Wright and the Scottish Avalanche Information Service. Particular thanks should go to Rory Stewart and Sue Kimber for helping with proof-reading at very short notice. Sorry if I have missed anyone!

In the process of talking to climbers about the routes outlined in this edition it has been interesting to note how many have disagreed on route grades, especially with some of the harder climbs. It is in the nature of the game that we play which is dictated by 'conditions' which cause some variance to the original line and difficulty. Winter guidebook details will always be much harder to follow than the summer rock climb with its clinical breakdown of moves and rock features. Such is the mystery and uncertainty of an ice/snow covered mountain. Hopefully this guide will lead climbers to the foot of the route and help them assess a way to the top. In between much will be left up to their experience and ability to handle different conditions en route.

In the final analysis the guidebook author must take the blame for incorrect or poor detail and obvious omissions. Please contact me with your criticisms or praise if it is felt necessary. Only by continuing feedback from the guidebook users will this guidebook to Britain's most important winter climbing area progress.

Good climbing,

Alan Kimber
Mountain Guide and guidebook author,
'Calluna' Heathercroft, Fort William.

A queue at the Great Tower on Tower Ridge

INTRODUCTION

Ben Nevis; the peaks of Glen Coe and the surrounding mountains give some of the best snow and ice climbing anywhere in Europe, when the conditions are right. So popular and well known is Ben Nevis, that in recent years climbers from as far afield as Poland, Australia, France, Italy and the USA have been seen trudging the delights of the 'famous' Allt a'Mhuilinn approach. Hamish MacInnes and Yvon Chouinard have made films of winter climbing on Ben Nevis, as have French guides, who continue to bring clients back each year. Justifiably a good 'tick' on any discerning world travellers' itinerary.

Budding mountaineers and climbers from the British Isles are fortunate in having these peaks so close, as they provide excellent training for people intending to visit the Alps or greater ranges of the world, whether climbing or trekking. Today's winter specialists will find more than enough climbing to the highest of modern technical standards to encourage them back, year after year.

Many of the routes are longer than experienced anywhere else in British hills and of alpine-like seriousness. It is not a good idea to be lured onto the famous 'Tower Ridge' of Ben Nevis as your first Scottish winter climb. The Lochaber Mountain Rescue Team have escorted dozens of shivering 'all nighters' off this route in the dull grey hours of dawn! Try something shorter to start with as a 'Wee Scottish Apprenticeship'.

A combination of short daylight hours and possible strong winds, poor weather and snow conditions add to the serious nature of Scottish winter climbing. Fitness is of prime importance to sustain climbers through long hours, carrying far more weight in their rucksacks than would be experienced in the summer months. Climbers must be economical with their time and aim to keep moving as fluently as is practical, in order to avoid a possibly serious 'benightment' or slip on a dark unknown descent. Records show that novice and experienced climbers alike come to grief on these Scottish mountains, sometimes with fatal consequences.

The winter season varies greatly. Generally the best months will be February, March and April, with some excellent conditions often appearing in April high on Ben Nevis, but not on the lower surrounding peaks. The first winter snows arrive in September, but often are short-lived in the moist Atlantic airstream. October and certainly November can provide good but lean climbing conditions early on. However, these months, along with the Christmas and New Year period are something of a lottery, with short daylight hours. The easier grade 1 gullies can often be climbed right through to June/July, especially on Ben Nevis where large patches of snow remain in the shadowy hollows all year round. Point Five Gully has been climbed as early as November and as late as May.

In compiling this guidebook for winter climbers visiting Ben Nevis and Glen Coe, the author, Alan Kimber has drawn on twenty-four years of experience gained from living in Fort William. During that period he has worked as both instructor and mountain guide with a variety of different organisations from private outdoor centres to national bodies for mountain training. Alongside this day to day work a deep sense of personal satisfaction and enjoyment has been gained from travelling and climbing amongst Britain's highest and most demanding peaks in winter.

As well as a deep understanding of the peaks in this guidebook, the author has gained from visits to the Himalayas, Peru, Alaska, Baffin Island, Labrador and Africa, plus numerous seasons in the European Alps. At present he runs his own mountain training and guiding company based in Fort William.

WEATHER AND AVALANCHES

The area covered by this guidebook is well known as having some of the most severe weather in the British Isles. A combination of strong winds and snowfall coupled with fluctuating temperatures provide the climber with potential life-threatening situations of a varied nature. Before setting out on any climb it is wise for climbers to inform themselves of the likely snow and weather conditions they are likely to meet.

In response to the steadily increasing number of avalanche incidents, the Scottish Sports Council through The Scottish Avalanche Information Service funds daily snow observations in the Northern Cairngorms (Northern Corries and Loch Avon Basin), Glen Coe and Glen Etive, and Lochaber (Ben Nevis to Aonach Mor). Specially trained, experienced mountaineers monitor and report on snow conditions and avalanche risk on a daily basis throughout the winter. Comparative studies of snowpack structure are increasing our understanding of the nature and cause of avalanches in these popular mountain areas.

A snow conditions and avalanche report is prepared each day and made available to the public through the national media as well as local outlets. Through these reports it is hoped to provide the climber, walker and off-piste skier with up to date, reliable information on snow conditions, avalanche danger and the effect of weather on these. This will aid the mountain user in making decisions regarding route choice in planning a safe and enjoyable excursion into the hills.

It cannot be stated too strongly that even the most sophisticated forecast is only an adjunct to the range of information available to the mountaineer. It is not a substitute for good judgement but rather an aid to better judgement.

Snow and Avalanche Reports
Reports are prepared every day and are available from:

MOUNTAIN CALL	East:	01898 500 442
	West:	01898 500 441
CLIMB LINE	East Highlands:	01898 654 668
	West Highlands:	01898 654 669

POLICE AVALANCHE
INFORMATION LINE   01463 713191

Radio and television news bulletins, notice-boards and other strategic locations in the Glen Coe, Cairngorm and Lochaber areas.

Avalanche Awareness
BEFORE SETTING OUT

1. Seek expert local advice. Avalanches can have certain characteristics which are peculiar to one area. Even experienced mountaineers can benefit from local knowledge.
2. Get the most recent snow and avalanche report and weather forecast.

3. Find out about the weather during the past week. How has this affected snow conditions? Will the forecast weather increase or decrease the risk of avalanches?

4. Be prepared to modify your plans in the light of this information.

ON ROUTE

5. The most reliable indicator of avalanche danger is signs of recent avalanche activity. Is this confined to slopes of a particular orientation?

6. Observe the condition of the snow as you go along:

   Is there evidence of drifting?

   Wind Slab is the most common type of avalanche!

   How deep is the new snow?

   The deeper the snow, the greater the stress and therefore the danger.

   Is it getting warmer or colder?

   A sudden change in temperature is a common trigger.

   Cold weather prolongs avalanche risk.

   A rapid thaw of unconsolidated snow causes wet avalanches.

7. Have a close look at the surface layer of snow where the majority of avalanches occur. Use your axe or ski to dig through this layer to the one below. *How firmly does the surface layer adhere to the one below?* If it breaks away easily then all slopes of similar aspect and altitude should be avoided.

8. Follow a line which avoids suspect slopes and the possibility of being swept onto rocks should a slide occur.

If You Witness an Avalanche

* OBSERVE the victim's progress and mark both the starting point and the point at which last seen.

* CHECK for further avalanche danger.

* Make a THOROUGH SEARCH of the debris surface:
   - LOOK for any sign of victims
   - LISTEN for any sounds
   - SEARCH the most likely burial spots

* Make a SYSTEMATIC SEARCH, probing the debris with axes

or ski poles with baskets removed.
* If a victim is recovered, administer FIRST AID.
* Send someone for help.

If You are Caught in an Avalanche

* An initial loud shout may help in letting others know of your problem. Do not continue to shout too much as snow entering the lungs can cause serious damage. In fact it is a good idea to keep your mouth shut most of the time.
* Try and delay your slide by digging into the underlying base on which the avalanche is sliding. This is only practical if the avalanche is a shallow one. Also it may be possible to hold onto rocks or trees.
* Try and keep your head uphill and stay on your back with arms outstretched in a wide backstroke swimming motion.
* Jettison your rucksack, as it can pull you down into the snowpack.
* A final supreme effort as the avalanche slows will hopefully bring you to the surface or create an airspace.
* Good luck!

Recommended Reading

A Chance in a Million by Barton and Wright, pub. Scottish Mountaineering Trust.

Mountaincraft and Leadership by Langmuir, pub. Scottish Sports Council and Mountain Leader Training Board.

Avalanche Safety for Climbers and Skiers (Daffern).

Using the Snow and Avalanche Report

LOOK AT:

* Date and time of issue. Information for the report is gathered as late as feasible during the day.
* Avalanche hazard for day of issue. The hazard quoted for day of issue reflects conditions found at that time. This states the hazard on a 5 point scale from Low (1) to Very High (5). It includes a general statement, noting highest risk areas and details of observed avalanches. Hazard figure quoted refers to highest risk areas.

* Avalanche outlook for the day following day of issue. This includes a numerical hazard scale outlook. This will be correct IF THE WEATHER FORECAST IS CORRECT. If the weather FORECAST is inaccurate, you must use your own judgement to assess the effect on avalanche risk.

EUROPEAN AVALANCHE HAZARD SCALE		
Degree of hazard	**Snowpack stability**	**Avalanche probability**
1 Low	The snowpack is generally well bonded and stable.	Triggering possible only with high additional loads** on a few very steep extreme slopes. Only a few small natural avalanches (sluffs) possible.
2. Moderate	The snowpack is moderately well bonded on some* steep slopes, otherwise generally well bonded.	Triggering is possible with high additional loads** particularly on the steep slopes indicated in the bulletin. Large natural avalanches not likely.
3. Considerable	The snowpack is moderately to weakly bonded on many* steep slopes.	Triggering possible, sometimes even with low additional loads**. The bulletin may indicate many slopes which are particularly affected in certain conditions, medium and occasionally large-sized natural avalanches may occur.
4. High	The snowpack is weakly bonded in most* places.	Triggering probable even with low additional loads** on many steep slopes.
5. Very High	The snowpack is generally weakly bonded and largely unstable.	In some conditions, frequent medium or large-sized natural avalanches are likely. Numerous large natural avalanches are likely, even in moderately steep terrain.

* Generally described in more detail in the avalanche bulletin (e.g. altitude, aspect, type of terrain etc

** additional load: - high: e.g. group of skiers, piste machine, avalanche blasting)

- low: e.g. skier, walker

- steep slopes: slopes with an incline of more than 30 degrees

- steep extreme slopes: particularly unfavourable in terms of the incline, terrain profile, proximity to ridge, smoothness of underlying ground surface.

aspect: compass bearing directly down slope

natural: without human assistance

NOTE: Cornice collapse is a specialised type of avalanche, often independent of general avalanche risk. When cornice danger is known to exist, it will be specified.

Thanks to Blyth Wright and Scottish Avalanche Information Service for supplying details relating to avalanche assessment.

EQUIPMENT AND SAFETY PRECAUTIONS

Map and Compass

This guidebook will hopefully help climbers to find their route. It must be used in conjunction with a weather-proof map. All the areas in this guide are covered by the:

O.S. Landranger series, Sheet 41, Ben Nevis, Fort William and surrounding area, 1:50,000.

Ben Nevis, The Aonachs and Stob Ban are also covered on the O.S. Outdoor Leisure 32, Mountainmaster, Ben Nevis, the Grey Corries and the Mamores, 1:25,000 map. This is a very useful map with a 1:10,000 insert of the Ben Nevis plateau area and is essential for use with this guidebook.

The ability to use these maps with a compass is of prime importance to all winter mountaineers and climbers.

Ice Axe/Hammer/Crampons

Ice axe and crampons are essential for any winter outing, whether walking or climbing. For climbing it is assumed that two tools (axe and hammer) are used, either drooped pick or inclined (banana) model. Many good tools are available and the first-time buyer might consider a modular system which allows new picks to be fitted at a reduced cost when compared to buying a complete axe/hammer. Tools should be 50/55cm in length for climbing.

Boots

Stiff plastic boots with well maintained vibram sole are best for winter climbing and when linked to a pair of clip-on crampons provide a solid and positive base for the necessary footwork involved in climbing snow and ice.

15

Helmet

A climbing helmet is recommended, especially when climbing below other parties who may be dislodging large brick-sized lumps of ice from above.

Climbing Protection

For protection on steep ground, rock pegs should be carried along with the full array of more modern chocks and equipment. Be aware though that too much gear weighs you down and slows the day. Only take what is required for the route, e.g. Tower Ridge does not require ice screws or dead-men, whilst Point Five will. I well remember seeing a party of climbers in Gardyloo Gully (Grade 1 at the time) festooned with every gadget available, from 'Friends' to 'Wallnuts'. The nearest rock was buried under three metres of snow and they did not have a dead-man with them. A 50m rope is recommended.

Body Comforts

Food and spare clothing should be carried - light thermal layers are far better than chunky sweaters and duvets. Try and keep the weight to a minimum. A sensible balance between lightness and safety is required. A bivvy bag should be considered as it will certainly come in handy one day along with a headtorch and spare battery and bulb.

NOTES ON THE USE OF THIS GUIDE

Gradings

..."*Much debate has taken place over the years concerning the grading of Scottish winter climbs. It continues to bubble and boil and will no doubt still be without a solid foundation when the next guidebook is published!*"...This was the statement on grades in the last (4th) edition of this book. Much has happened since then and we now have a two-tier system, courtesy of the Scottish Mountaineering Club which appears to suit the current crop of climbers. This guide has adopted that system and the method for using it has been copied below in large parts verbatim from the new SMC Ben Nevis guidebook in order that some consistency is maintained. If, like the author of this guide you prefer a single number, climbers are advised to choose the biggest one. This in effect gives a traditional extended grading system. If you are in the apparent minority who would like to see Scottish grades lowered to suit the French system, you are advised to emigrate for the time being at least! At the time of going to press Glen Coe did not have a complete two-tier system and most routes will reflect the original traditional system with only the harder climbs showing the new method.

Some significant climbers have expressed dismay at the new system and have asked for the original grades to be shown. The original grades are shown in the index of route names along with any stars.

It has become apparent whilst compiling this guidebook that different climbers in different areas are interpreting the new system in different ways. For instance the harder climbs in Glen Coe are receiving a higher Roman numeral (seriousness) even though they are shorter and better protected than the ice routes on Ben Nevis which have long unprotected run-outs and therefore should be receiving a higher seriousness rating when compared to the better protection on snowed up rock climbs. Even ice climbs such as Elliot's Downfall (VII,5) in Glen Coe appear to be overgraded when compared to The Shroud (VII,6). The first route is one pitch and can be descended by abseil from a tree, whilst the second climb is five pitches long and at one point ascends a free-hanging icicle employing a semi-hanging stance on ice screws followed by an ascent of a large (often avalanche prone) corrie. By comparison Elliot's Downfall should be no more than VI,5/6.

Any climbers wishing to offer opinions on the new system should contact the SMC (Scottish Mountaineering Club). As in previous systems the difficulty of a climb increases with a higher number. The grades of I and II can be considered as introductory, whilst only experienced climbers should attempt grades higher than this.

The grades are for average conditions and it should be remembered that winter climbs can vary enormously from time to time, depending on snow or ice build-up and the weather. Early in the season when conditions can be lean, certain routes will be harder than later on when a good plating of ice covers blank stretches, making them easier. Also it must be remembered that the passage of a mild weather system over the whole of the area covered by this guide will change the character and difficulty of many climbs overnight.

Winter climbs have been graded using the two-tier system, in which the Roman numeral indicates the overall difficulty of the climb and the accompanying Arabic numeral represents the technical difficulty of the hardest sections of climbing.

The aim of the two-tier system is to grade modern mixed routes to indicate their high levels of technical difficulty, while taking into consideration the frequently greater seriousness of the older style ice routes.

(i)   Nearly all grades up to and including grade IV retain their original overall grades.

(ii)   Climbs of grade IV and above (and some of grade III) have two grades, an overall grade in Roman numerals, and a technical grade in Arabic numerals.

(iii)   The overall grade takes into account all factors affecting the difficulty of reaching the top of the climb, including its technical difficulty, seriousness (frequency of protection and reliability of belays) and sustainedness (length of hard sections of climbing and number of hard pitches).

(iv)   The technical grade reflects the actual difficulty of the hardest section(s) of climbing, without reference to seriousness. It is not intended to be used as a technical pitch-by-pitch grading. On a climb of overall grade V, a technical grade of 5 indicates relatively straightforward, steep ice climbing; a technical grade of 6 generally indicates more technical mixed climbing; technical grades of 7 and 8 indicate much more intricate and harder snowed-up rock moves.

(v)   The technical grade normally varies by not more than two below or two above the overall grade. Thus V,5 can be taken as an average grade V route of the old system. A higher technical grade than the overall grade would indicate greater technical difficulty, offset by better protection (as frequently found on mixed routes); a lower technical grade would indicate greater seriousness. Thus the system has some parallels with the E-grade system for summer rock climbs.

(vi)   The previous artificial ceiling of grade V (and reluctant VI) has been removed, so as to reflect more realistically the differences between the old classic climbs of grade V and the current state-of-the-art routes.

(vii)   The overall difficulty is reflected in the overall grade, and just as an E1 5a can be a more serious proposition than an E1 5c, a V4 is not necessarily easier overall than a V6.

Some degree of variability undoubtedly occurs according to the prevailing conditions. While some climbs will nearly always be possible at close to the given grade, others require special (or even extraordinary) ice build-up, and the grades apply to such favourable situations. At other times these climbs may simply be non-existent. Although the two-tier grading system is new, the grades given to the climbs in this guidebook have been decided after extensive consultation.

A complete list of the new grades for all harder Scottish winter climbs in this and other areas (where information is available) has been published in the 1992 SMC Journal.

N.B. A split grade such as II/III indicates the possibility of a wide variation in difficulties depending on conditions.

Length of Climb
Length of climbs and where possible pitch lengths are given in metres. Route lengths are as accurate as possible and will hopefully give the climber at least a reasonable idea of the scale of the route.

Recommended Routes
Where possible a three star system has been used to indicate quality under good conditions, the more stars the better the route. However, many routes under good conditions would warrant some special mention. The star system will hopefully allow strangers to the area to find some good climbing on their first visit. Difficulty is not a pre-requisite for stars and many simple climbs get a mention on the basis of their character, continuity, structure and adventure at the grade. All very subjective!

Diagram & Route Numbers
Nearly all cliffs have a diagram but for those without, the text is sufficient to locate a route. Not all routes are shown (numbered) on

the diagrams in order to avoid overcrowding. The routes numbered offer good reference points for adjacent non-numbered climbs. If a climb is shown on a diagram the page number of that diagram will be shown at the end of the route description.

RESCUE FACILITIES

The Mountain Rescue teams of Lochaber and Glen Coe (civilian volunteers) attend more call-outs than all the other Scottish teams put together. Along with the RAF (helicopter and land-based teams) they provide an excellent service. They are experienced and skilful local mountaineers who undergo regular training in mountaineering and remote care first-aid skills. Rescues are co-ordinated by the Police, who should be contacted on 999 in case of an accident or possible problem. DO NOT DELAY IN RAISING THE ALARM IF YOU FEEL SOMEBODY IS IN NEED OF HELP.

Public Telephones and M.R. Posts

Ben Nevis	Youth Hostel in Glen Nevis (GR 127717)
	Distillery (GR 125757)
	Golf Course Club House (GR 136762)
Glen Coe	Kingshouse Hotel
	(M.R. Post - GR 259546)
	Achnambeithach
	(M.R. Post - GR 140565)
	Clachaig Hotel (GR 128567)

For climbers on Ben Nevis a direct radio link with the Police in Fort William is situated in the small annexe on the left, outside the main entrance to the C.I.C. Hut. Open the door and lift up the large wooden flap in front of you. This will reveal a simple handset with a sprung switch built into it. Keep the switch depressed whilst asking for the Police. The following will be sufficient: ... Fort William Police ... Fort William Police ... this is C.I.C. Hut ... C.I.C. Hut ... Can you hear me? ... Release the handset/switch and wait for the Police to reply. Give your message. (Don't forget to depress the switch every time you speak and release it every time you want to listen. Should you get no reply, give your message anyway. Be clear and economical with what you say. Give brief details of where the accident has taken place (name the route), the nature of any injuries if known and how many people are involved. Stay by the radio until the rescue team arrives unless instructed otherwise.

On Ben Nevis at present three emergency shelters exist: Coire Leis - GR 173713; Carn Dearg NW - GR 158719: and on the summit of Ben Nevis. Of these three very small shelters the only one that is of any use as a shelter against the elements in winter is on Ben Nevis summit itself. The other two structures are very often buried under many feet of snow and filled full of spin-drift early in the winter. Do not rely on finding them and then spending much time and effort excavating them. That time and effort could easily be used to get off the hill.

As an aid to rescue (if it is required) climbers should consider leaving a note of their intended route with a reliable person in the valley. The Police will be happy to take a note for you so long as you "clock off" on your safe return!

AMENITIES

Fort William and Glencoe are well supplied with all the necessary facilities required by climbers.

Transport

Coaches travel daily from Glasgow, passing through Glen Coe en route. Trains arrive at Fort William daily and it is not unknown for climbers from London to catch the sleeper on a Friday evening, climb on Saturday and Sunday, then head back to work on the Sunday night train!

Glasgow or Inverness airports are both approximately two hours drive from Fort William with direct coach links.

Shops

Four specialist climbing shops can be found:

Glencoe Guides and Gear (GR 095586)
West Coast Outdoor Leisure, High Street, Fort William
Nevisport, High Street, Fort William
Brighams, Fort William (opposite the hospital).

Of particular interest to climbers coming down late are the Spar shops in Claggan (GR 117743) and Ballachulish (GR 083583), where all foodstuffs can be found to fill the hungriest belly. Fort William and the nearby village of Caol have 'chippies'. For the more discerning a visit to the Nevisport restaurant/bar will empty your pocket and fill your stomach. The Clachaig Hotel in Glen Coe provides good bar meals and beer for climbers. A large Safeway supermarket in Fort William stays open late most nights and has a cafeteria.

Cinema	Cameron Square, High Street, Fort William.
Hospital	The Belford Hospital (GR 106741).
Doctors	Fort William (01397) 703773/703136/702947
	Glencoe (01855) 811226.
Police Station	Fort William (01397) 702361
	Glencoe (01855) 811222.

Climbing Wall and Swimming Pool (GR 109742).

Avalanche & Weather Information
Local Climbing Shops, Nevisbank Hotel, Clachaig Hotel, Police and various lay-bys.

Accommodation
This section is intended to offer advice on accommodation for the whole area. Climbers visiting the area covered by this guide should have no problems finding places to rest their weary heads! Everything from five-star hotels to flooded campsites are available. The following is a small list of the selection available and reflects the style of accommodation which climbers generally appreciate (?)!

Calluna, Heathercroft, Fort William. Tel: Fort William (01397) 700451
Kingshouse Hotel and Bunkhouse. Tel: Kingshouse (018556) 259
Glen Nevis Youth Hostel. Tel: Fort William (01397) 702336
Glencoe Youth Hostel. Tel: Ballachulish (01855) 811219
Clachaig Hotel and Chalets. Tel: Ballachulish (01855) 811252
McColl's Bunkhouse and Cottage. Tel: Ballachulish (01855) 811256
Onich Inchree Chalets. Tel: Onich (01855) 821287
Snowgoose Holidays (Bunkhouse). Tel: Corpach (01397) 772467
Bunkhouse Kinloch Leven. Tel: Kinlochleven (018554) 471
Achintee Bunkhouse. Tel: Fort William (01397) 702240
Grey Corrie Lodge, Roy Bridge. Tel: Spean Bridge (01397) 712236
Aite Cruinnchidh, Roy Bridge. Tel: Spean Bridge (01397) 712315
Mamore Lodge, Kinlochleven. Tel: Kinlochleven (018554) 213

A number of climbing huts are available for bookings in the area

Comb Gully (IV, 4), Ben Nevis. Climber: John Taylor

from Crianlarich to Fort William. A complete list of these is available from the Mountaineering Council of Scotland, Tel: (01764) 654962. For a complete list of all types of accommodation, from hotels to campsites contact the Fort William and Lochaber Tourist Office, Tel: (01397) 703781 and ask for their accommodation guide. A glance through the back pages of most outdoor magazines will illuminate further possibilities.

Mountain Guides

For anyone wishing to hire the services of a member of the British Association of Mountain Guides in order to explore the climbs in this book in the company of a local expert, four local outfits offer a comprehensive service:

Alan Kimber (Professional Mountaineering Services) Tel: (01397) 700451
Paul Moores (Glencoe Guides and Gear) Tel: (01855) 811402
Mick Tighe (Nevis Guides) Tel: (01397) 712356
Bill Newton Tel: (01397) 712513

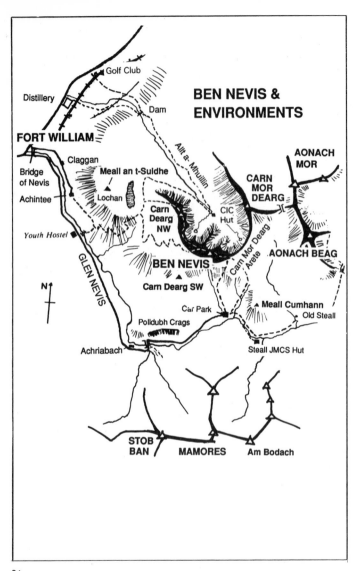

BEN NEVIS & ENVIRONMENTS

Golf Club
Distillery
Dam
Allt a. Mhuilinn
FORT WILLIAM
Claggan
Bridge of Nevis
Achintee
Meall an t-Suidhe
Lochan
Carn Dearg NW
CIC Hut
AONACH MOR
CARN MOR DEARG
AONACH BEAG
Youth Hostel
Carn Mor Dearg Arete
BEN NEVIS
Carn Dearg SW
GLEN NEVIS
N
Car Park
Polldubh Crags
▲ Meall Cumhann
Old Steall
Achriabach
Steall JMCS Hut
STOB BAN
MAMORES
Am Bodach

BEN NEVIS

APPROACHES FOR BEN NEVIS

Approaches for climbs on the N.E. aspect of Ben Nevis all aim initially for the C.I.C. Hut (GR 167722). This hut is private and belongs to the Scottish Mountaineering Club. At present bookings can be made through Bob Richardson, 2 Inch Lonaig Drive, Balloch, Glasgow, G83 8JH. (OS Map sheet 41 Ben Nevis 1:50,000 or OS Outdoor Leisure Map sheet 32 Mountain Master 1:25,000).

Distillery Approach

Parking is available near the Ben Nevis Distillery visitor centre (GR 124756). Entrance is made through the main gate and cars should be parked well away from the visitor centre towards the traffic lights. A donation to the local M.R. team can be made in return for this at the Distillery Office. The paths shown on the maps are accurate and lead in $1^1/2$-2 hours to the hut. Initially it is necessary to walk through the premises of the distillery before crossing the railway line and linking into the path system that leads up the hill. On striking a good motorable track (private) follow it to the dam (GR 147751). From this dam the path follows the east bank of the Allt a'Mhuilinn (boggy) to the hut.

Golf Club Approach

A slightly shorter route. Please keep off the greens at all times. Parking is available in the Golf Club car park (GR 136762). Please respect the main users of this facility; the golfers! One positive aspect of using this approach is that the Golf Club Bar is often open on returning to the valley, especially if you are late down! Walk through the tunnel under the railway and cross the golf course and walk up the east side of the stream following a good path which links in with the first approach, $1^1/2$ - 2 hours.

Glen Nevis Approach

The approach from the south-west follows the zig-zag 'Pony Track' (Tourist Route to the summit) as far as the broad saddle between Meall an t-Suidhe and the main massif of Carn Dearg NW, Ben Nevis. This track starts from Achintee Farm (GR 125729). A popular alternative is to start from the Youth Hostel in Glen Nevis (GR 127717) and climb steeply to join the main track. Access and parking is also available for the Pony Track route by the footbridge over the River Nevis (GR 123731).

Above the saddle which holds the large Lochan Meall an t-Suidhe (or 'Half-way Lochan', Grid Square 1472) the pony track veers back to the right (south), crosses the Red Burn, and zig-zags up the long slope to the summit plateau. Where the pony track swings to the south, the route to the hut branches off northwards. It follows an indefinite path contouring the lower slopes of Carn Dearg above the Half-way Lochan for about one km until it reaches the remains of an old fence on the lip of the Allt a'Mhuilinn glen. From this point it gradually descends for about 30m in a north-easterly direction and then continues traversing south-east across the hillside until it reaches the Allt a'Mhuilinn (500m below the C.I.C. Hut). A large boulder, the Lunching Stone, will be seen on the left of the path along this traverse. The route now follows the right bank of the Allt a'Mhuilinn burn until it is joined by another large stream coming in from the right (out of Coire na Ciste). This is crossed, and the hut, situated on the crest of a blunt spur between the streams, is about 100m above.

Starting from the youth hostel, this approach is only slightly longer than the route up the glen but in bad visibility the route-finding is more difficult and after a big snowfall the saddle and traverse into the glen are very prone to heavy drifting and possible avalanche below the Castle area, 2-2^{1}/$_{2}$ hours.

Other approaches to the North-East face: there are two alternative variations (with little to choose between them) starting from the large car park at the end of the Glen Nevis road. Both are exceptionally steep and are unsuitable for use as a means of reaching the C.I.C. Hut and not recommended for reaching the majority of climbs. But in good visibility for the fit valley-based climber, they give the quickest approach to the Little Brenva Face or the normal route on North-East Buttress.

(a)   From the car park take a diagonal line up the hillside to reach the saddle between Meall Cumhann and Ben Nevis and then follow the ridge in a north-westerly direction. Finally, when the steep ridge merges into the easier angled slopes above, veer slightly right to gain the Carn Mor Dearg Arête at the Abseil Post Sign (GR 171710) (2-2$^{1}/_{2}$ hours). Descend into Coire Leis by the easiest line. If approaching routes on the Little Brenva Face, a traverse left from the col leads in five minutes to the foot of 'Bob Run'. Beware of avalanches on this traverse line.

(b)   Climb straight up above the car park follow the bank (right-east) of the waterslide of Allt Coire Eoghainn. Once over the lip of the Coire, head up to the right (north-east) to join the previous route on the ridge 200m below the Carn Mor Dearg Arête (2-2$^{1}/_{2}$ hours). Care should be exercised on this route as many fatal accidents have occurred on the slabs at the top of the waterslide.

(c)   From the Steall Hut the best way is to join route (a) at the Meall Cumhann saddle. Follow a small indefinite track which leaves upper Glen Nevis immediately above the entrance to the gorge, and makes a rising traverse above it, crossing the flank of Meall Cumhann until it is possible to strike up to the saddle. Alternatively one may follow the Allt Coire Guibhsachan (above the ruin of the old Steall GR 186687), by the left (west) bank and head directly up the westward branch corrie to gain the Carn Mor Dearg Arête. However, there are great areas of slab in this corrie which can be very difficult under icy conditions. Also descent from the Carn Mor Dearg Arête into Coire Leis is difficult and only recommended from the Abseil Post Sign area.

DESCENTS FROM BEN NEVIS

(See front end paper map)

The high summit plateau of Ben Nevis is surrounded on nearly all sides by steep and difficult ground. Many accidents have occurred in descent. Often this part of the day will call for more concentration and shrewdness of judgement than at any other time.

The best descent will be determined not only by your point of arrival on the summit plateau but also by the weather and snow conditions. The shortest way will not necessarily be the best and in really bad conditions the only safe way off the mountain may be by Route 1 below; long and tiresome though it may be. Careful use of map and compass and the sketch plan of the cliffs given in this guidebook will suffice to get you down but local knowledge is invaluable. When visibility is good, make a close study of the general topography of the mountain and if possible visit the summit plateau with a view to memorising its details and recording important compass bearings. The ruined observatory, topped by a survival shelter, is an unmistakable landmark on the summit itself even though the neighbouring triangulation point and numerous cairns may be obliterated in a hard winter.

The best aids to descending from the summit of Ben Nevis are the O.S. Map, Outdoor Leisure 32, Mountainmaster of Ben Nevis, 1:25,000 and a compass, and the ability to use both in vile weather conditions. These two items should form essential companions to this guidebook. The insert on the map (Scale 1:10,000) is particularly useful. It shows the sharply indented plateau, and the gullies which must be avoided on compass bearings in poor visibility.

Anyone who visits the mountains in summer or winter without a map and a compass (and the ability to use them in 'white out') is putting their life at risk.

Using the map previously mentioned the following descents are recommended:

1. Red Burn

The easiest and safest way down the mountain. Follow a grid bearing of 231° for 150m from the summit (use a rope to measure it if you are not sure how many double paces you take to 100m). This will avoid the steep drop of Gardyloo Gully close on your right. Then follow a bearing of 281° (grid). Don't forget to convert your grid bearings to magnetic (approx. +5° in 1994). On this last bearing you should reach continuously steeper ground after 800m of down hill travel. At this point the 'Tourist' route meets the plateau. Continue on down an easy slope, for another kilometre on the same bearing, then turn north towards 'Halfway-Lochan'.

N.B. Along this route it is important not to stray left (south) in the first 2km, as this would lead to the steep and serious ground of 'Five Finger Gully'. The steep lip of this gully is also 800m from the top of Gardyloo Gully. Accurate pacing and compass work is an essential skill for all people climbing on Ben Nevis. If after 800m on the recommended bearing you encounter steep ground and cliffs dead ahead you are advised to try and avoid them by going right until it is possible to continue on the bearing (281 deg grid). This may require that you travel uphill for a short distance to skirt the top of 'Five Finger Gully'.

IF YOU FINISH UP HEADING SOUTH DOWNHILL AND SKIRTING THE TOP OF STEEP CLIFFS ON YOUR RIGHT AFTER 800m FROM THE TOP OF GARDYLOO GULLY IT IS HIGHLY LIKELY THAT YOU HAVE MADE A NAVIGATION ERROR AND ARE VERY CLOSE TO 'FIVE FINGER GULLY'. GO BACK UPHILL UNTIL IT IS POSSIBLE TO CONTINUE ON THE ORIGINAL BEARING (281 deg grid).

The Red Burn is well known as a good 'Bum Slide'. Please be aware that large waterfalls exist at the bottom of the burn before it reaches the track and many large rocks are present all the way up the burn which will not only rip your expensive Goretex pants, but may put a hole in your head as well! This area does avalanche from time to time also.

2. No.4 Gully

For climbers returning to the C.I.C. Hut or Allt a'Mhuilinn area, this descent is straightforward in good visibility. The top of the gully has a metal marker post with the number 4 drilled into it (GR 158717). Sometimes the cornice can be impassable, but a slot is usually dug out from below. Also it is possible at times to move a few metres to the north, along the rim and gain access to the gully down steeper ground. Avalanches have occurred in this gully from time to time and the initial entry can be steep, but it soon eases. Take care.

N.B. A bearing due west from the lip of this gully (270° grid) is a descent to Glen Nevis, via the Red Burn mentioned previously.

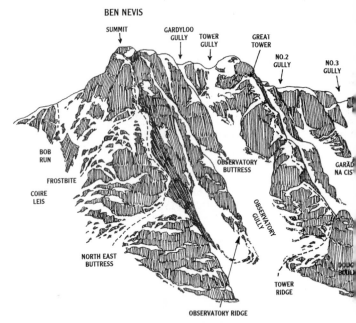

GENERAL VIEW FROM CARN MOR DEARG

3. Carn Mor Dearg Arête/Abseil Post Sign

This route can be used with care. It provides a method of descending quickly to a lower altitude, especially if the weather on the plateau is fierce. MANY DEATHS HAVE OCCURRED ON THIS DESCENT OVER THE YEARS. Most of the fatalities have been connected with people straying too far left (north) from the summit on descent.

From the summit trig point a bearing of 134° (grid) should be held. Initially the ground will be flat. After 100m the gradient steepens abruptly and some short posts may be seen; keep these to

30

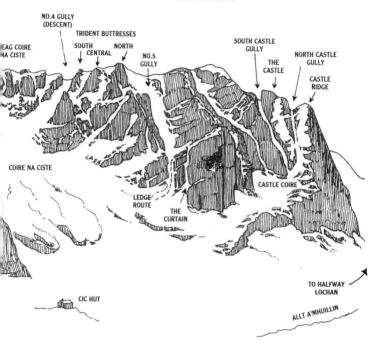

CARN DEARG NW

your left (north-east). From the steepening after approximately 200m of descent a slight col will be found to the left (east) half a kilometre from the summit. At this point is a metal sign (GR 171710) with information relating to the 'Abseil Posts'. Only two of these posts remain (winter 1994) and with care the person experienced in negotiating Grade 1 ground in descent will be able to move down easily but steeply into Coire Leis. Often it is easier to traverse left (west) towards the Little Brenva Face, before descending. However, snow build-up will dictate the easiest and most obvious route down. The angle is steep at first, but eases after 150m. As with many snowy descents be careful after strong winds during periods of heavy drifting to avoid being another avalanche victim on this slope.

N.B. From the Abseil Post Sign it is possible to descend to the head of Glen Nevis on a bearing of 220° (grid). This leads to the top of the 'Waterslide' mentioned elsewhere under approaches. The original bearing of 134° (grid) from the summit should not be followed for more than 500m as it leads to steep and dangerous ground.

Extra Tips:

For those climbers 'topping out' on the following routes in poor visibility and not wishing to visit the summit, these bearings will help:

Tower Ridge	214° grid for 130m then 281° grid to Red Burn
Tower Gully	214° grid For 50m then 281° grid to Red Burn
Gardyloo Buttress	214° grid for 75m then 281° grid to Red Burn
No.2 Gully	281° grid to Red Burn
No.3 Gully	281° grid to Red Burn
Green/Comb Gully	220° grid for 150m then 281° grid to Red Burn

For climbers finishing on routes to the east of the summit (N.E. Buttress and Little Brenva Face) it is advisable to try and find the summit as a definite reference point before descending if they are unsure about the descent. To do this, it should be possible to use the N.E. edge of the plateau above Zero, Point Five and Hadrian's Wall as a 'handrail' to the summit. Cornice collapse has caused a few fatalities in this area so stay roped, with only one member of the party near the edge.

BEN NEVIS - GENERAL TOPOGRAPHY

The northerly faces of Ben Nevis and Carn Dearg N.W. (see diagram p30/31) form one continuous complex of cliffs which attain a maximum height of 500m and extend for 3½kms overlooking the upper part of the Allt a'Mhuilinn glen. It is the most impressive

Brenva Face, Moonwalk (III/IV). Climber: Klaus Schwartz

First ascent of Gemini, Direct Start (V)
Climber: Alex McIntyre   Photo: Alan Kimber

First pitch of Point Five Gully (V)
Climber: George Grassam   Photo: Alan Kimber

mountain face in the British Isles. The incomparable classic ridges are flanked by formidable walls leading back into deeply recessed corries which themselves contain numerous large buttresses and gullies. The scale is so vast that it is difficult to appreciate, particularly on first acquaintance.

Walking up the glen of the Allt a'Mhuilinn, the first feature the climber will see on the right is Castle Ridge and its flanking North Wall. Beyond this and at a higher level is the recess of Castle Corrie which contains the Castle itself, its two demarcating gullies and to the left of these the tapering pillar of Raeburn's Buttress. The cliffs then jut out again. The left-hand side of the Castle Corrie is known as the North Wall of Carn Dearg; this cliff connects with a 300m prow of compact rock, a truncated spur, the Great Buttress of Carn Dearg. Waterfall Gully is the dividing line between these last two. Round the corner of the Great Buttress is No.5 Gully, set at a reasonable angle but almost 500m in length. Ledge Route comes out of No.5 Gully to gain the crest of the ridge at the top of the Great Buttress and follows this to the summit of Carn Dearg. To the left (east) of the Great Buttress the cliffs fall back to form the great amphitheatre of Coire na Ciste, the floor of which at over 900m is a wild and magnificent place to visit. There are three relatively easy exits from the head of the corrie; No.4 Gully (hidden) on the right; No.3 Gully apparently the lowest col in the centre and No.2 Gully which disappears to the left of the prominent buttress of the Comb. Tower Ridge is the next main feature and is one of the most important on the mountain. Narrow and very long, it projects for $1^1/2$ kms from the summit plateau into the glen to terminate abruptly as the Douglas Boulder immediately above the hut. From the foot of the boulder (215m in itself!) there is a vertical rise of over 550m before the junction with the plateau.

To the east of Tower Ridge is the long slope of Observatory Gully which branches in its upper quarter to form Gardyloo and Tower Gullies. Observatory Gully, broad in its lower part and tapering as it rises for 500m is only an approach to other climbs and can be regarded almost as a deep corrie. Rising to the left of the gully are some of the most formidable climbs on the mountain: The Minus Gullies and Buttresses and the Orion Face (all on the flank of North

33

East Buttress); Zero Gully which lies in the corner between Orion Face and the long spur of Observatory Ridge and finally Point Five Gully and Observatory Buttress.

The final great ridge almost at the head of the glen is called the North East Buttress. It is again a massive projection, almost 500m in vertical height, but is steeper and therefore not as long as Tower Ridge. Below the First Platform it terminates in a great rock nose not unlike the Douglas Boulder. The Allt a'Mhuilinn glen ends in Coire Leis below the col of the Carn Mor Dearg Arête. Overlooking this corrie is the east flank of the North East Buttress; now generally referred to as the Little Brenva Face.

The climbs are described from east to west (left to right) corrie by corrie.

CLIMBS FROM COIRE LEIS

Coire Leis is the basin at the head of the Allt a'Mhuilinn glen. From the C.I.C. Hut follow the right bank of the burn until opposite the lowest rocks below the First Platform of North East Buttress, then traverse up the right-hand side of the corrie beneath the east face (about 1 hour from the C.I.C. Hut).

Although all the routes on the Little Brenva follow fairly arbitrary lines they are very popular. The face is alpine in character, receives the full benefit of any sun and consequently often becomes heavily iced. Generally the climbs are long and give some interesting route finding; considerable difficulty may be experienced in misty conditions.

Final Buttress   55m   III
At the extreme left side of the face is a short buttress. Climb an ice pitch in the centre.

Bob-run   130m   II
I. Clough, D. Pipes, H. Fisher, B. Small, J. Porter & F. Jones 10th February 1959
Commences almost at the level of the col of the Carn Mor Dearg Arête and follows a couloir in the left extremity of the face. Start to the right of a buttress and climb 30m of ice or iced rocks to gain the

LITTLE BRENVA FACE

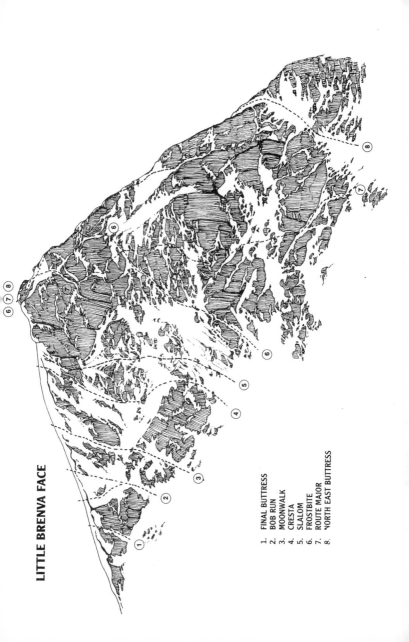

1. FINAL BUTTRESS
2. BOB RUN
3. MOONWALK
4. CRESTA
5. SLALOM
6. FROSTBITE
7. ROUTE MAJOR
8. NORTH EAST BUTTRESS

couloir. After another 30m the route curls round to the left by either of two variations, both of which generally give at least one further pitch on ice.

Moonwalk   270m   IV,3**
K. Hughes and J. Mothersele   March 1973
Start 10m left of Cresta below an ice pitch which can vary in difficulty depending on conditions. Climb the ice above and continue over a snow slope to the foot of an ice pitch formed by a rock corner (100m). Climb the ice above to another snow slope (45m). Move up to a steep ice wall (45m). Climb this for 15m and an ice groove to snow-ice field (35m). Cross rightwards to belay below rock wall (45m). Traverse horizontally right below the wall to a steep rock arête which is followed to the summit slopes.
N.B. Many variations are possible in this area and escapes left (south) can be made with care towards Bob-Run.

Cresta   275m   III**
T.W. Patey, L.S. Lovat and A.G. Nichol   16th February 1957
The main feature of this route is a 180m shallow couloir which commences above and to the left of a rocky spur and finishes amongst the small cliffs at the exit from the highest part of the left-hand side of the face. The original start was from the right but it is now more usual to commence to the left of the rocky spur and about 30m right of Bob-Run. 30m of icy rocks (or ice) are climbed to gain a long broad snow shelf. A small gully leads up from the right-hand side of the shelf to reach the couloir proper which is followed to its termination in an ice basin. Traverse up to the right to gain an easy snow slope which leads out to a finish about 50m from the top of N.E. Buttress. A direct finish has been climbed through the exit cliffs (*M. Slesser and N. Tennent, 18th February 1957, IV,4*)

Slalom   275m   III**
D. Pipes, I. Clough, J.M. Alexander, R. Shaw and A. Flegg   6th January 1959
The upper part of the right-hand side of the face is a steep rock wall, the Central Spur. Both Slalom and Frostbite start in the bay below

this wall and to the right of a rocky spur.

Slalom starts up a shallow tongue of snow from the left of the bay and zig-zags up through the rock bluffs towards the middle of the wall of the Central Spur. Below the Spur a long rising leftwards traverse is made to gain an easy snow slope which leads to the foot of a rocky ridge overlooking the couloir of Cresta. The rocks usually give the crux of the climb and lead to the final easy exit slope which is shared with Cresta.

Frostbite   275m   III
I. Clough, D. Pipes, J.M. Alexander, P.A. Hannon and M. Bucke February 1958
Starts from the above mentioned bay and follows an icy groove up to the right to gain a 120m snow field. Follow this rightwards and cross a rocky ridge below the nose of the Central Spur proper to gain further snow slopes slanting rightwards under the Spur. These eventually lead out onto the crest of the N.E. Buttress below the Mantrap, (see N.E. Buttress Route).

Route Major   300m   IV,3***
H. MacInnes and I. Clough   16th February 1969
Not an easy route to find and follow, but for those people who enjoy exploring middle grade mixed ground, an excellent route when in condition. The route generally follows the line of a summer climb (Eastern Climb). To get a good look at the route it is advisable to walk up the east side of Coire Leis above the hut until opposite the start of N.E. Buttress. A hanging ice-field high on the face is a key feature towards which climbers should aim. A start from the traverse line (left end) onto the First Platform of N.E. Buttress can be made. Follow ice ribs up the wall to gain a snow slope crossed by Frostbite. Cross this and continue up the buttress by a chimney line going right (difficult route finding). Where the route goes close to the Mantrap of N.E. Buttress break out left on a horizontal traverse then up various small snowfields to the top.
N.B. An alternative start to the climb can be made by walking up directly under N.E. Buttress and continuing until the ground levels out as it approaches upper Coire Leis. From here turn up right and commence climbing. This start is well right of Frostbite.

North East Buttress 350m IV,4***
W.W. Naismith, W. Brunskill, A.B. Kennedy, W.W. King and F.C. Squance April 1896
The normal winter route avoids the rocks below the First Platform by going up into Coire Leis until a broad easy shelf leads back up to the right to the First Platform. Shortly above the Platform the rocks on the crest become very steep and the easiest route is to traverse an exposed ledge on the right until a gully leads back up to the left to reach the small Second Platform. Alternatively the steep step may be turned on the left or even taken direct. Above the Second Platform the ridge is followed, turning obstacles, until a smooth blunt 5m nose bars the way. This is the notorious Mantrap which can be extremely difficult in icy conditions. It is best turned on the right by a slight descent and traverse to a scoop. This leads to the foot of a steep corner which again can be very hard. It may be best to move slightly down to the left until, not far above the top of the Mantrap, a shallow chimney leads up to the left of the ridge crest on to easier ground. This upper part of the route is normally the crux of the climb, but the major difficulties are relatively short and it is not too far to the top; probably better to force the route than be faced with the long retreat.

Newbigging's Route - Far Right Variation 180m IV,4**
R. Campbell, R. Carrington and J.R. Marshall February 1972
This route is on the triangular face which falls vertically into Coire Leis as one walks beneath the First Platform of N.E. Buttress. It starts 10m left of the rocky edge of the face (this edge forms the north and east facets of the buttress) and runs parallel to that edge. The route is a natural winter line and easily seen on approaching the hut. Follow the big corner groove and slabs, passing an overhang on the left. The main difficulties are in the lower 60m. In lean conditions with poor icing this route can be serious. Rarely in condition.

Raeburn's Arête 230m IV,5***
D.F. Lang & C. Stead 25th January 1986.
Follows the arête formed by the north and east facets of the first platform of N.E. Buttress. A good climb which is not often in

condition. Go right below the first overhang to a deep groove which is climbed to a belay (45m). Follow grooves up slightly right then go left beneath another overhang to a block belay on the edge (100m). Follow the arête more easily to the top of the first platform (90m).

CLIMBS FROM OBSERVATORY GULLY

Very large avalanches fall from the upper reaches of this gully. It would be wise to avoid the climbs at the top end of this gully during or after heavy snowfall, strong winds or during a thaw.

Beneath the First Platform of N.E. Buttress and to the left of Slingsby's Chimney is a considerable area of steep ground, easily seen on the hut approach up the Allt a'Mhuilinn. The following four routes are located in this area and when in condition provide good sport at a lower level.

Green Hollow Route   200m   IV,4*
J.R. Marshall and J. Moriarty   February 1965
Start at the lowest rocks on the left (often snow-covered) and trend diagonally up rightwards by iced slabs and grooves towards a large snow bay, high up in the middle of the face, The Green Hollow. From the highest point of the bay climb an iced slab left onto the final arête. Follow this easily to the top of the First Platform.

Bayonet Route   185m   III
I. Griffiths, E. Jackson & C. Stead   7th March 1982
Start mid-way between Raeburn's Arête and Slingsby's Chimney. Follow a steep icy groove direct towards an overhang. Gain and climb the rib on the left of the overhang, then traverse left onto the arête.

Ruddy Rocks   180m   IV,4
J.R. Marshall, R. Marshall & R.N. Campbell   March 1967
Starts immediately right of Bayonet Route. Climb towards twin chimney-cracks to the right of the large overhang. Follow the cracks and grooves to easier ground and continue to a small overhang which is turned on the right. Easy ground upwards to the First Platform.

Raeburn's 18 Minute Route   140m   II
E.U.M.C. Party   March 1952
Start 6m left of Slingsby's Chimney and follow the line of least resistance to the First Platform.

Slingsby's Chimney   125m   II/III
C. Donaldson & J. Russell   April 1950
A direct approach to the First Platform of N.E. Buttress from the west. To the right of the slabby rocks of the nose leading to the First Platform is an obvious shallow gully fault. This gives the climb.

THE MINUS AND ORION FACES

To the right of Slingsby's Chimney is a steep area of cliff. It is split by three gullies (the Minus Gullies: Minus 3 on the left) and bounded on the right by Zero Gully.

MINUS THREE BUTTRESS

Lies between Slingsby's Chimney and Minus Three Gully. All routes escapable.

Right-hand Wall Route   140m   IV,5
R. Ferguson and J. Higham   March 1972
Just to the right of Slingsby's Chimney is a line of chimneys: follow this line as close as possible, the final slabby part below the First Platform giving the crux.

Slab Rib Variation   150m   IV,5*
C.D. Grant & C. Stead   22nd March 1982
Climbs the rib immediately right of Slingsby's Chimney.

Wagroochimsla   140m   IV,5
S. Docherty and G. Adam   January 1972
Start between Right-hand Wall Route and Platform's Rib and climb left to the central bulge; climbed with aid on first ascent. Continue rightwards to the Second Platform.

Platform's Rib   150m   IV,4*
H. MacInnes, I. Clough, T. Sullivan and M. White   8th March 1959
Follow the rib to the left of Minus Three Gully until part of the gully
is used before moving back left to the North East Buttress.

Minus Three Gully   160m   IV,4***
R. Smith and J. Marshall   7th February 1960
When in condition, a classic. Climb steep snow to a cave belay, climb
steep ice on the left and continue by a groove to snow. Another steep
pitch leads to easier climbing and North East Buttress.

MINUS TWO BUTTRESS

To the right of Minus Three Gully is a slabby buttress, interrupted
at about one third height by overhangs and forming a prominent
ridge on the left. Bounded to the right by Minus Two Gully.

Left-hand Route   270m   VI,6**
S. Docherty and N. Muir   30th January 1972
A delicate climb on thinly iced slabs. Start immediately right of
Minus Three Gully and ascend the huge groove/corner for 60m
passing an overhanging section. Steep ice leads to an easier section
of slabby rocks and eventually to Second Platform.

Central Route   270m   VI,7
A. Nisbet and B. Sprunt   18th March 1979
The climb follows a line just to the right of the previous route
following the raised crest on the front face to the overhangs. These
are gained by a rightward traverse and turned on the right using aid
to reach easier ground.
N.B. First ascent took a very long time! Rarely if ever repeated.

Right-hand Route   270m   VI,6*
R. Carrington and A. Rouse   March 1972
To the right of the prominent ridge is a large slabby corner. Climb
the large corner (or just to the right), then a short more difficult
corner to gain the easier angled upper section of the buttress with
difficulty. Slabs and grooves lead to the North East Buttress.

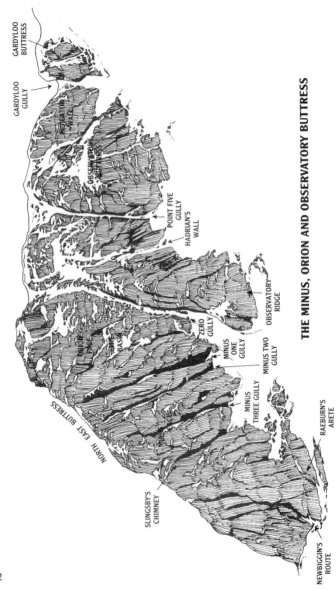

THE MINUS, ORION AND OBSERVATORY BUTTRESS

GARDYLOO BUTTRESS

GARDYLOO GULLY

OBSERVATORY BUTTRESS

TOWER GULLY

POINT FIVE GULLY

HADRIAN'S WALL

OBSERVATORY RIDGE

ZERO GULLY

ORION FACE

BASIN

MINUS ONE GULLY

MINUS TWO GULLY

NORTH EAST BUTTRESS

MINUS THREE GULLY

SLINGSBY'S CHIMNEY

RAEBURN'S ARETE

NEWBIGGIN'S ROUTE

N. E. Buttress, Ben Nevis

Minus Two Buttress   270m   V,5*
B. Dunn, C. Higgins and D. McArthur   5th March 1974
Start 13m to the left of Minus Two Gully and go up an icefall then right to an open book corner. Climb all of the corner to a prominent snow crest. Traverse a snow ramp leftwards and climb an iced gully line to the North East Buttress.

Minus Two Gully   270m   V,5***
J. Marshall, J. Stenhouse and D. Haston   11th February 1959
A fine climb when in condition. A long pitch of snow and ice leads to a belay below an overhang. Avoid the overhang by a detour to the left and regain the upper chimneys leading to the North East Buttress. The initial chimney can be avoided by thin iced slabs 2m to the left.

MINUS ONE BUTTRESS

The narrow buttress to the right of Minus Two Gully and bounded on its right by Minus One Gully.

Minus One Buttress   290m   VI,6***
N. Muir and A. Paul   5th April 1977
Start at the centre of the buttress, at a corner, and follow the easiest line to the overhangs at 100m. Move across rightwards and follow the buttress, fairly close to Minus One Gully to the North East Buttress. Fine open buttress climbing.

Minus One Gully   290m   VI,6***
K. Crocket and C. Stead   23rd February 1974
The hardest of the Nevis gullies. Easy climbing leads to an ice wall giving access to a cave below the main overhang. Avoid the overhang on the left before regaining the gully above. Continue past a snow bay to the North East Buttress.

THE ORION FACE

This area of the mountain lies immediately left of Zero Gully. On its left and lower down is the toe of the buttress which takes the line of Astronomy. This buttress projects into the approach slopes leading

THE MINUS AND ORION FACES

1. SLINGSBY'S CHIMNEY
2. PLATFORM'S RIB
3. -3 GULLY
4. LEFT HAND ROUTE
5. -2 BUTTRESS
6. -2 GULLY
7. -1 BUTTRESS
8. -1 GULLY
9. ASTRONOMY
10. URBAN SPACEMAN
11. ORION FACE DIRECT
12. ASTRAL HIGHWAY
13. JOURNEY INTO SPACE
14. SLAV ROUTE
15. ZERO GULLY
16. OBSERVATORY RIDGE

45

to Orion Face. The bottom of the face is a steep icefall with the Great Slab Rib to the left. Above and right of this rib is an obvious feature known as The Basin. At the top left side of The Basin is a steep icy exit known as Epsilon Chimney. Up right of this Basin is the Second Slab Rib which is often the only feature showing in the middle of the face when snow and ice obliterate all other detail. Higher up is another smaller basin snow patch and left of this at a higher level, the exit chimney.

Astronomy   300m   VI,5***
H. MacInnes, A. Fyffe and K. Spence   March 1970
Start about 16m to the right of Minus One Gully and climb twin cracks to leftward slanting snow patches. These snow patches lead to a groove. Climb the groove and go right to a large corner. Up the corner then move right, then back left by walls and grooves. Skirt left below the upper rocks and escape by descending into the top of Minus One Gully (or follow the next route which gives a better finish).

Astronomy, Direct Finish 120m   VI,5**
C. Fraser & M. Thompson   16th February 1986
Instead of skirting left below the upper rocks into Minus One Gully, trend slightly right to belay below the right-hand end of the steep upper rocks. Gain the crest of the buttress on the right and climb an iced slab, trending right to gain a fine ice groove near the crest of the buttress. Follow this steeply to easier ground. Less often in condition compared to other routes on the Orion Face.

   (Author's note: Tim Jepson and Roger Baxter-Jones climbed a similar line in the late seventies.)

The Black Hole   235m   VI,6**
A. Saunders & M. Fowler   5th April 1986
Starts 15m left of Orion Direct. Climb an awkward right-facing corner to gain the left side of the Great Slab Rib (50m). Follow the corner on the left side of the rib for 30m, then move left to an obvious ice-choked overhanging crack which is climbed to a snow patch (45m). Climb the overhanging fault line above to belay at the top left

of another snow patch (35m). Move back right into the fault line which is climbed to join Astronomy where it traverses left into Minus One Gully (45m). Another couple of pitches in the same line up thinly iced grooves (60m). Much of this route had been climbed previously.

Urban Spaceman   350m   VII,6***
D. Hawthorn & A. Paul   12th April 1983
Start at the same point as Orion Direct and move up left to below the Great Slab Rib (35m) which is followed on the crest to a stance (30m). Continue on a similar line to a belay (40m). Reach a set of open grooves up right (30m) and follow them to beneath the steep upper section (50m). Move over slabs up right to a stance (30m). Follow a steep ice-filled chimney which overlooks the Basin, then steep mixed ground (45m). A further 90m leads to N. E. Buttress. An excellent route but not often in good condition.

Smith-Holt Route   420m   V,5**
R. Smith and R. Holt   January 1959
Starts left of Orion Direct and climbs leftward facing corners immediately left of the Great Slab Rib, until it is possible to cut back right into The Basin with difficulty. From The Basin the steep and icy Epsilon Chimney is taken and exit made easily via a ledge leading up left to the crest of N.E. Buttress at a 'V' notch. A great route which avoids the queues on Orion Direct.

Orion Direct   420m   V,5***
R. Smith and J. Marshall   13th February 1960
A classic: the technical difficulty is often low but in such conditions belays are usually poor. Climb to the left end of a broad ledge stretching out from Zero Gully and take a steep chimney line above until an upward traverse left leads to The Basin. It is possible to continue direct to The Basin from the chimney but harder. Move up rightwards to an obvious rock rib (Second Slab Rib) and take this by the face to the right, or by a longer traverse right below the face. Trend up leftwards in three pitches to finish in the steep icy exit chimneys.

On Orion Direct (V). Climbers seen in the background are on Zero Gully (V). Climber: Alan Kimber

A direct route in two pitches of steep sustained ice is possible to reach the Basin (V,5** *S. Docherty & N. Muir, March 1971*)

Astral Highway   240m   VI,5***
C. Higgins and A. Kimber   28th December 1976
A direct finish from The Basin starting at the top of The Basin, left of centre at the groove right of Epsilon Chimney. Gain the groove and climb it and successive grooves to reach the North East Buttress above the 40 foot corner.

Zybernaught   240m   VI,5
D. Hawthorn and A. Paul
Follows a set of zig-zag grooves between Epsilon Chimney and Astral Highway. From the foot of Epsilon Chimney move up right and below steep bulge (45m). Climb bulge and ground above to left trending groove (45m). Follow groove to open corner (45m). Climb corner and ground above to North East Buttress.

Journey into Space   240m   VII,6**
A. Kimber and C. Higgins   8th March 1980
Start midway between Astral Highway and Second Slab Rib. Climb
directly to the right of a short corner where a delicate traverse right
gives easier climbing. Climb diagonally leftwards by an obvious
iced slab until a break right can be made onto the upper section of
the wall. Climb slab, move right beneath overhang then by groove
direct, climbing occasional bulge until right end of prominent
snowfield is reached. Move diagonally left up snowfield (possible
to finish direct) and climb obvious corner to finish.

Long Climb Finish   240m   VII,6**
A. Cain & R. Clothier   March 1983
A steep alternative finish to Orion Direct which follows steep icy
grooves just left of the Second Slab Rib.

Slav Route   420m   VI,5***
D. Lang and N. Quinn   23rd March 1974
Takes a line just to the left of Zero Gully, but completely independent.
An obvious icefall at 50m is climbed direct or possibly avoided to
the left. Near the top an exit can be made into Zero Gully but a better
line slightly leftwards is taken to an obvious open corner up left of
the gully.

Zero Gully   300m   V,4***
H. MacInnes, A. Nichol and T. Patey   18th February 1957
The easiest but most serious of the big three classics: the lack of
belays meriting the V grade. Climb the gully to a stance below a left
facing chimney to the left of the main gully. Ascend the chimney
then traverse right to an amphitheatre in the gully. Take the narrow
gully above to easy ground by a long pitch.
N.B. An alternative start can be made to Zero Gully by climbing the
steep ice on the right, thus avoiding the rightward traverse higher
up. This option varies with conditions. Also, as with many other
steep gully lines Zero is not a nice place to be when breezes on the
summit deposit vast quantities of powder snow down the climb!
Beware of debris from other parties.

OBSERVATORY RIDGE

The ridge itself is the narrow buttress to the right of Zero Gully but as an area is taken to stretch to Point Five Gully.

East Face　　　　　166m　　IV,5*
B. Dunn and C. Higgins　3rd March 1974
Below and to the right of Zero Gully, the left side of Observatory Ridge is split by a line of grooves which give the route, until they merge into the ridge itself.

Silverside　　　　　115m　　IV,4*
B. Dunn and D. Gardner　17th April 1977
Start 16m below East Face and move up rightwards over snow and iced grooves to the left end of a large ledge. Traverse left and climb left slanting line to a snow bay and easier ground.
N.B. The above two climbs finish up the following route.

Observatory Ridge　　　420m　　IV,4***
H. Raeburn, F. Goggs and W. Mounsey　April 1920
The finest and most difficult of the classic ridges, the line of the route generally follows the crest of the ridge. The lowest buttress normally gives the most serious problems. The easiest line is to gain a shelf on the left flank one third of the way up this buttress and then work obliquely rightwards to the crest. Above this difficulties can be turned and the upper part of Zero Gully is often taken for the final 150m.

The following routes lie on the right (west) wall of Observatory Ridge overlooking Observatory Gully and the approach to Point Five Gully.

Observatory Wall　　　90m　　IV,4
D. Hawthorn and A. Paul　November 1985
A crackline left of Abacus has been climbed. It has a cave at half-height. Climb to the cave by slabs and exit left and up cracks to the crest of the ridge.

Abacus   106m   IV,4*
N. Muir and A. Paul   27th November 1977
The route climbs the obvious bow-shaped chimney groove in the
middle of the face between Observatory Ridge and Hadrian's Wall
to reach the ridge.

Antonine Wall   150m   IV,4*
N. Muir and A. Paul   3rd December 1977
Just right of Abacus is a steep ice-filled groove leading to a slab
capped by a huge roof. Climb the groove to below the roof and move
right over slabs to a snow groove leading to the crest.
N.B. The last three routes are good bad weather routes, as it is
possible to descend by abseil as did the first ascentionists.

West Face Lower Route   325m   IV,5**
W.D. Brooker, J.R. Marshall, T.W. Patey   1st February 1959
Start as for Vade Mecum (next description) and climb to twin ice
grooves. Follow the left-hand groove to a steep snow bay beneath
vertical rock walls. Traverse right beneath the walls to enter a deep
icy chimney. This chimney leads to the easier upper section and a
variety of plateau exits which include Observatory Ridge or Zero
Gully on the left. The route is also known as Hadrian's Wall.

Vade Mecum   320m   V,5**
D. Knowles, D. Wilson and party   1974
Start just left of the ice-smear of Hadrian's Wall Direct, and climb
over slabby mixed ground to an obvious pointed block. Move left
and finish by a steep ice-pillar to Observatory Ridge.

Hadrian's Wall Direct   320m   V,5***
M. Geddes and G. Little   April 1971
Between Observatory Ridge and Point Five Gully is a very obvious
ice-smear. Nowhere steep, this popular climb is rather poorly
protected lower down (poor belay stance after first pitch). Climb the
smear in two or three pitches to a chimney with good belay. Take the
chimney to a snow patch and gain Observatory Ridge after two long
pitches.

ZERO GULLY

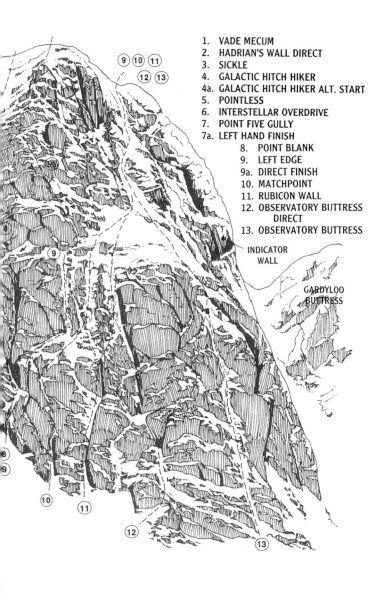

1. VADE MECUM
2. HADRIAN'S WALL DIRECT
3. SICKLE
4. GALACTIC HITCH HIKER
4a. GALACTIC HITCH HIKER ALT. START
5. POINTLESS
6. INTERSTELLAR OVERDRIVE
7. POINT FIVE GULLY
7a. LEFT HAND FINISH
8. POINT BLANK
9. LEFT EDGE
9a. DIRECT FINISH
10. MATCHPOINT
11. RUBICON WALL
12. OBSERVATORY BUTTRESS DIRECT
13. OBSERVATORY BUTTRESS

INDICATOR WALL

GARDYLOO BUTTRESS

Sickle 300m V,5***
B. Hall and M. Geddes December 1977
Start to the right of Hadrian's Wall Direct and move up leftwards to climb a groove parallel with, and close to, Hadrian's Wall Direct; then go back right to continue by a steep ice corner to join Hadrian's Wall Direct at the snow patch, just above the chimney.

Galactic Hitchhiker 300m VI,5**
M. Geddes and C. Higgins 14th April 1978
One of the first Grade VI's climbed on Ben Nevis. Right of Hadrian's Wall Direct the main feature is the rightward stepped corner system above the great slab left of Point Five. Climb just left of the centre of the slab to a small nose (50m). Move up right into the main groove system beneath the corner. Traverse right above the slab in an exposed position via a pointed block to belay on the right. Continue above by very steep and difficult walls and ledges right of the main corner system to easier ground which is followed to the top.
N.B. An easier start (V,5) can be made on the left and nearer to Sickle, followed by a traverse right to a pointed block.

Pointless 300m VII,6*
N. Banks and G. Smith 19th February 1978
A difficult climb, especially on the second pitch. Start on the obvious slab close to the left side of Point Five Gully. Follow the right edge of the slab towards a rock barrier which is level with the normal first belay of Point Five Gully (bottom of the chimney). Trend up left at the rock barrier to a spike belay beneath a steep obvious corner (50m). Climb the corner with difficulty (possible peg on left wall) and trend right at the top. Continue directly for two interesting (III) pitches. Easier climbing leads in three pitches to the plateau rim. A variation start (*VI,5 50m M.Fowler & A.V. Saunders 29th March 1986*) can be made by climbing a short corner from the foot of Point Five Gully (8m) followed by a traverse left above the prominent steep slab to the foot of the difficult second pitch.
N.B. As with many ice climbs the first pitch of this route may be longer if the build-up at the base of the cliff is lacking.

Interstellar Overdrive   300m   VI,5*
I. Kennedy and R. Anderson   March 1980
Climb the left-hand rib of Point Five to belay below a wall (30m). Go
right across the wall until immediately above Point Five. Follow a
groove running left to a chimney, which is the right side of an
enormous perched block. Climb the chimney to a belay on top of the
block (40m). Climb a corner and ice wall (crux) rightwards above to
a ledge in a snow bay (40m), followed by a groove on the right,
which trends back left to meet Pointless above the difficult section
(40m).

Point Five Gully   325m   V,5***
I. Clough, D. Pipes, R. Shaw and J. Alexander   12th-16th January 1959
A justifiably popular route. The standard Grade V from which all
other steep snow/ice gully climbs are gauged. The main difficulties
are encountered on the first three pitches. A left trending slab of ice
leads to good belays on the left beneath a steep chimney (45m).
Climb the steep chimney to an overhung recess, belay on the right
(45m). Follow the gully above easily with one steeper section (II/III)
to pass the cornice on the right. Beware of falling debris from other
parties and spindrift avalanches.
N.B. For climbers on top form and requiring more excitement, it is
recommended that they take to the left wall of the gully after the
third hard pitch. Find your own way to the top at about Grade IV,4
depending on the line chosen.
    An escape rightwards is possible (III) onto the Girdle Traverse
ledge running towards Good Friday Climb. Move out right from
beneath the last hard pitch (pitch 3).

OBSERVATORY BUTTRESS

This is the final, upper part of the great left wall of Observatory
Gully. It stretches rightwards from Point Five Gully to Gardyloo
Gully (which forms the obvious exit gully at the top left of
Observatory Gully). From the foot of Gardyloo Gully an initially
broad terrace cuts leftwards across the upper part of Observatory
Buttress, narrowing as it goes. The face above the right side of this
terrace is called Indicator Wall: the face being bounded on the left
by the short gully of Good Friday Climb.

Pointblank   325m   VII,6***
M. Duff and J. Tinker   4th March 1984
(Direct version 2nd ascent, as described)
M. Duff and R. Nowack   24th February 1988
Climbs the buttress immediately right of Point Five Gully. Start 4m
below the foot of Point Five and climb a small steep groove left of
Left Edge Route to the snow patch of that route. From the left edge
of the snow patch move up right to corner and belay (25m). Climb
the right-hand groove/crack above and thin icy slabs to a corner
and capping roof. Semi-hanging stance on pegs (22m). 3m below the
stance on the right enter a short groove which is climbed to a narrow
chimney crack. Follow this crack to a roof and go diagonally left till
overlooking Point Five Gully. Climb directly via a steep groovy
ramp and wall to a snow bay and ledge system. Belay on rounded
spike (43m).
N.B. It is possible to avoid the hanging stance on the second pitch
and thus arrive at the snow bay, by using a 70m rope as did the 2nd
ascent party. Right of the belay climb a sloping groove and more
easily above to a series of steps (40m). Follow a series of indistinct
corners and steps to the crest on the right of Point Five Gully. The
upper section of this climb and small parts of the lower pitches had
previously been climbed by Dave Wilkinson on a variant ascent of
Left Edge Route.

Left Edge Route   360m   V,5*
D. Lang and N. Quinn   9th March 1974
Start at the foot of Point Five gully and climb a rib to a snow patch.
Climb the left-hand groove above then move up right to an ice-fall
which is followed to the terrace. Either move right along the terrace
and finish by Ordinary Route (see below) or move back left near the
terrace and follow the fine snow arête.

Matchpoint   325m   VI,6*
S. Richardson and E. Hart   29th March 1986
Between Left Edge and Rubicon Wall are two left facing corner
systems. Climb the right-hand one (50m). Climb a short steep snow
slope to an overhanging, inverted triangular wall. Traverse left and

climb an icicle fringe to a snowfield. Climb the right-hand icefall above to the terrace (the left-hand one being on Left Edge Route), and continue up the buttress as for Left Edge Route Direct finish.

Rubicon Wall 340m V,5**
N. Muir and A. Paul 14th April 1977
A prominent icefall forming in a left-facing corner gives the line of this good route, taking three pitches to the Girdle Traverse ledge. Start about 20m right of Left Edge Route and take a more or less direct line up to the terrace. Finish as for Left Edge Route.

Direct Route 340m IV,4**
D. Stewart and W. Foster 23rd March 1952
Ascend rightwards on snow patches and short walls, starting not far to the right of Rubicon Wall, to join Ordinary Route above its main difficulties.

Ordinary Route 340m V,5***
J. Marshall and R. Smith February 1960
In good conditions an obvious narrow icefall forms on the right side of the buttress. Start well to the right of Direct Route below a chimney some way up the buttress. Climb the buttress by a shallow depression to reach the chimney which usually gives the crux. From the terrace above the chimney go up leftwards to gain the final easy crest.

North-West Face 100m IV,4*
K. Crocket and C. Stead 21st March 1975
Start half-way up the right-hand side of the buttress at a bay and follow a chimney line leading to Indicator Wall, for which this route provides a good start.

Two more lines can be made to the right of North West Face climb. The first is 25m right of that route (50m V,6) and the second easier climb (30m III) takes a corner-groove at the right end of the buttress.

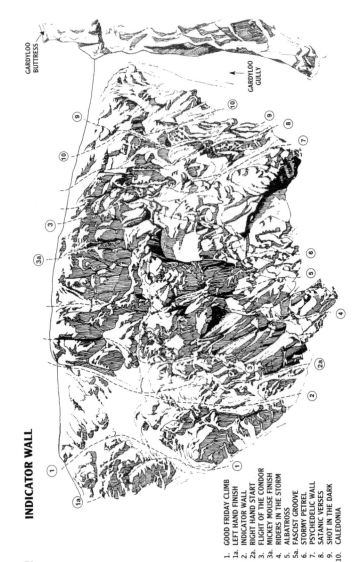

INDICATOR WALL

GARDYLOO BUTTRESS

GARDYLOO GULLY

1. GOOD FRIDAY CLIMB
1a. LEFT HAND FINISH
2. INDICATOR WALL
2a. RIGHT HAND START
3. FLIGHT OF THE CONDOR
3a. MICKEY MOUSE FINISH
4. RIDERS IN THE STORM
5. ALBATROSS
5a. FASCIST GROOVE
6. STORMY PETREL
7. PSYCHEDELIC WALL
8. SATANIC VERSES
9. SHOT IN THE DARK
10. CALEDONIA

Indicator Wall area, Ben Nevis

INDICATOR WALL

As described in the introduction to Observatory Buttress, Indicator Wall lies above the terrace cutting the upper part of Observatory Buttress, bounded on the left by the upper gullies of Good Friday Climb and on the right by Gardyloo Gully.

Ice climbs here are the highest in the British Isles starting at 1,200m. They are fine routes when in condition and well worth the long walk. Be prepared for poorly protected leads on steep ground!

Good Friday Climb   150m   III**
G. MacPhee, R. Lovel, H. Shepherd and D. Edwards   7th April 1939
Start below Gardyloo Gully and traverse left along the snow shelf until a gully can be followed for 60m where it is blocked by a wall. Go right then back left up another gully to the plateau. A possible left-hand finish (90m III,4) can be made from the top of the initial gully by climbing the rock wall direct and trending left above.

Indicator Wall   180m   V,4***
G. Smith and T. King   February 1975
About 50m right of the gully of Good Friday is an obvious icefall on the left side of the buttress. Start at an iced-chimney groove and climb bulging ice to snow slopes topped by a gully. Climb the gully to finish at the indicator post. A **Right-Hand Variant** *(160m V,5**. D.F. Lang & N.W. Quinn February, 1975)* is steeper and more direct. Start 15m right of the original route.

Flight of the Condor   200m   VI,5**
S.M. Richardson & J. Ashbridge   17th April 1993
Start as for Indicator Wall and climb a ramp to the groove of the right-hand variant (20m) then a short icy wall to gain the buttress crest on the right. Follow a groove to the left of a prominent block, then up and right to a stance below the slabby groove of Riders in the Storm (45m). Follow grooves until level with the stepped rightward line cutting across the face (25m). Descend and cross Albatross, continuing right. Thinly iced slabs at 25m lead to the upper traverse line which is followed to its end (45m). Continue moving right then up on thin slabs to below an overhanging

chimney. Step down right from the base of the chimney to a stance below and left of the final chimney of Stormy Petrel (45m). Ascend the ice wall above (15m), then on to the top (30m). A steep alternative finish is possible by following the corner that cuts through the headwall between Albatross and Stormy Petrel. Start at the end of the third pitch of the previous climb. *(Mickey Mouse Finish 50m VI,6 R. Clothier & D. McGimpsey, 17th April 1993)*

Riders in the Storm   165m   VI,5***
D. Hawthorn and E. Todd   April 1986
Climb the obvious buttress to the right of Indicator Wall by a series of corners and stepped icy grooves. Start just to the left of the lowest point of the buttress.

Albatross   150m   VII,6***
C. Higgins and M. Geddes   21st January 1978
A very open corner descends the face of the buttress about mid-way between Indicator Wall and Psychedelic Wall. Start slightly right of the main line and climb a groove for a pitch; then move back left to the main corner line. Follow this. An alternative start is possible by climbing a groove above the top left-hand corner of the snowy bay at the foot of the route. Climb the groove to a belay at a slab below an overhang (25m). Move up right into a narrow groove above the overlap on the second pitch of Albatross (30m). *(Fascist Groove 55m VI,6*, C. Rice & R. Webb, 12th February 1983)*

Stormy Petrel   160m   VII,6***
D. Cuthbertson and R. Kane   1982
A serious route with poor protection. Climbs the big open corner right of Albatross. Climb rightwards up a shallow ramp, then direct to a rock spike beneath an overlap (30m). Go right horizontally over ribs to belay at the roof of an impressive corner (21m). Climb the left wall of the corner to large slab above. Ascend steeply right in two pitches over slabs, corners and grooves (crux), turning a roof on the right. Belay at the foot of another corner (39m & 15m). Climb the corner then go left weaving through bulges and right to a shallow chimney and on to the final slopes, just left of Psychedelic Wall.

Psychedelic Wall   180m   VI,5***
N. Muir and A. Paul   January 1978
A direct line starting from the rocks, opposite the lowest rocks of the left edge of Gardyloo Buttress. Climb iced rocks to a snow bay (30m). Continue up steeply to gain a left trending snow ramp and from near its top take a groove leading to the left edge of a large plinth (45m). Continue up slabs, corners and chimney to the foot of a steep wall (36m & 30m). Climb the right-most of three corners to a cornice finish (39m).
N.B. On the second pitch it is possible to climb direct until 5m below an icicle fringe (belay). Climb to the icicle fringe, step left and follow ice to the top.

Satanic Verses   115m   V,5
C. Cartwright & R. Clothier   7th April 1989
Start immediately right of Psychedelic Wall and climb the left-hand of four parallel ramps which rise up right across the slabby wall. Climb to a second snow patch at 50m. Ascend grooves directly to a large snow bay (35m), belay. Climb the steep left wall and grooves above to the cornice which may be overcome to the left if it is too large at the approach point.

Shot in the Dark   120m   V,5**
M. Geddes and A. Rouse   11th February 1978
On the left wall of Gardyloo Gully 30m up from the toe of the buttress and right of Psychedelic Wall route. Aim initially for the oblong roof high on the wall above. Cross several rightward slanting overlapping grooves to a short corner. Climb this then traverse right across another groove and steep slab to finish some distance right of the oblong roof.

Caledonia   150m   V,5**
D. Gardner and A. Paul   18th February 1978
Climbs the steep slab corner about 60m up right of Psychedelic Wall, to gain a snow bay. Move up rightward trending snow ramp and steep slabs above, turning bulges on the right. This route finishes a little left of Shot in the Dark, left of the oblong roof.

Smith's Route (V,5), Gardyloo Buttress, Ben Nevis
Climbers: Andy Nisbet & Ken Crocket

Gardyloo Gully   170m II/III**
G. Hastings and W.P. Haskett-Smith 26th April 1897
One of the most popular routes on the mountain. The obvious direct
continuation to **Observatory Gully.** Normally a snow slope leads to
a great chockstone about 40m below the cornice. Sometimes there
is a tunnel beneath the chockstone which leads to a short, steep ice
pitch but in exceptional winters the whole route banks out. The
cornice can be difficult.

GARDYLOO BUTTRESS

This buttress tops Observatory Gully between Gardyloo Gully on
the left and Tower Gully on the right. The cornices can be very
considerable above this buttress and may be impossible to breach at
times.

Shot in the Light   100m IV,5
A.V. Saunders & P. Thornhill 1983
Climb the first break on the right, 50m up Gardyloo Gully, initially
up right to a belay (40m) then delicately back up left.

Left Edge   155m VI,5*
R. Carrington and A. Rouse March 1976
This route requires a very good plating of ice and snow. A peg for
tension was used high up to gain the upper slabs.
  Start at the left edge of the buttress and climb the arête up
rightwards until level with the upper chute of Smith's Route to the
right (100m). Move across to the chute and finish up this.

Kellett's Route   120m VI,6***
A. Paul and K. Leinster 1980
The most obvious line up the buttress is the leftwards slanting
icefall of Smith's Route leading to a snow chute in the upper part.
Kellett's Route starts midway between Left Edge and this icefall and
climbs directly to join Smith's Route (left-hand way) just below the
chute.

Comb Gully (III/IV), Climber: Trevor Jones   Photo: Alan Kimber
Looking down the crux pitch of Point Five Gully (V)
Climber: Nick Halls   Photo: Alan Kimber

GARDYLOO BUTTRESS

1. LEFT EDGE ROUTE
2. KELLETT'S ROUTE
3. SMITH'S ROUTE
3a. SMITH'S ROUTE ICICLE VARIATION
4. THE GREAT GLEN
5. RIGHT EDGE

In the exit chimneys of Orion Face Direct (V) Climber: Nick Halls

65

Augean Alley 120m V,5 (top section)**
K. Leinster, A. Paul and G. Reilly March 1981
This route climbs Kellett's Route (see above) and finishes on the left-hand ridge bounding the finish of Smith's Route.

Smith's Route 130m V,5***
R. Smith and J. Marshall 8th February 1960
Climb leftwards up the obvious slanting ice grooves to a belay. Move diagonally leftwards to easier ground then back up and right to the right-hand groove. Up this to the snow chute and an easy finish. A more popular variation is to climb an icicle direct to gain the right-hand groove, which is followed to the snow chute (*V,5. K.V. Crocket & C. Gilmore February 1975*). If the cornice is very large it may be possible to avoid it to the left by a steep wall and narrow ridge finish.

The Great Glen 130m VI,5*
P. Braithwaite and P. Moores 12th February 1978
The route follows the steep, shallow groove right of Smith's Route to exit left across a gangway to belay right of Smith's Route (51m). Re-enter the groove and follow steep arête on the right to snow. (Serious - take a long rope).

Right Edge 130m III*
R. Millward and F. von Gemert January 1977
Move up from the start of The Great Glen rightwards to gain the right arête of the buttress. Follow this to the top.

Tower Gully 120m I
G. Hastings, E.L.W. and W.P. Haskett-Smith 25th April 1897
Follow a broad snow terrace rightwards from the foot of Gardyloo Gully, below the buttress and above Tower Scoop to gain the gully proper. This is easy but the cornice is often large.

TOWER RIDGE EAST SIDE
The following climbs lie on the East Side of Tower Ridge starting from Observatory Gully.

Tower Scoop (III), Observatory Gully, Ben Nevis
Climber: Frank Trzebiatowski

Tower Scoop   65m   III***
I. Clough and G. Grandison   11th January 1961
Below the snow terrace which runs from the foot of Gardyloo Gully,
beneath Gardyloo Buttress to Tower Gully, is a band of icy cliffs
which almost block off Observatory Gully at 1,150m. The route
follows a central ice smear in two or three pitches. Various exits are
possible at the top.
N.B. To the left of this ice smear various short lines are possible, and
a little harder than Tower Scoop.

Tower Cleft   75m   III**
G. Pratt and J. Francis   February 1949
To the right of Tower Scoop is a deep cave-like rift formed in the
angle with the east flank of Tower Ridge. This rift is the line of the
route and can be very entertaining or impossible! (Move out left to
escape from the rift).

Clefthanger   90m   V,6**
D. Hawthorn and A. Paul   January 1985
Start at the foot of Tower Cleft and climb a corner system on the right wall. Climb 20m to a large ledge below a corner. Traverse right round an arête into a clean corner which is climbed passing a large dubious flake half-way on the left. Move up left by slabs, chimney and grooves.

East Wall Route   110m   II/III
J.R. Marshall and R. Marshall   February 1966
Starts just downhill and to the right of Tower Cleft. Climb one or two pitches to a snow ledge beneath a steep wall. Traverse right on steep snow to join the crest of Tower Ridge.

Echo Traverse   135m   III
J.R. Marshall & R. Marshall   February 1966
Follow East Wall Route until below a recessed chimney. Take a groove on the left to a spike (6m) and traverse left on thin slabs to a chimney groove which is climbed to a snow bay. Continue above in a left-trending fault to the ridge below The Great Tower. A direct icefall start is possible *(50m IV,4 A. Paul & P. Moores 22nd March 1992)*

The Great Chimney   65m   IV,5***
J.R. Marshall & R. Smith   6th February 1960
Climbs the obvious deep chimney which arrives on the ridge 50m below the Little Tower. Ascend the chimney past a belay under a vertical block then take the left crack and walls to the ridge.

Chimney Groove   90m   IV,6
C. Stead & D. Lang   27th February 1993
From the foot of The Great Chimney go right and up to a flake belay below a bulge which is climbed with difficulty to easier ground. The bulge may be avoidable on the right depending on conditions

Lower East Wall Route   125m   III
K.V. Crocket & C. Gilmore   25th March 1974

Start 60m down from The Great Chimney, climb a short overhang and follow ledges rightwards to the ridge above the first steep section.

The Tower Ridge   600m - 1¹/₂kms in length   Grade III***
J.N. Collie, G.A. Solly and J. Collier   30th March 1894
This, the most famous of the great Nevis ridges, is a magnificent expedition. Technically easier than the North East Buttress or Observatory Ridge, it should not be underrated. The main difficulties are concentrated high up and the whole route is exceptionally long and arduous.

The normal winter route avoids the face of the Douglas Boulder by entering the foot of Observatory Gully to the left and then cutting back right to climb the East Gully to Douglas Gap (I). An alternative start is via the Douglas Gap West Gully (I). From the gap a 20m groove/chimney leads to the crest of the ridge which rises gently and becomes quite narrow. It is possible to reach this section and avoid the moves out of the Douglas Gap by traversing in from higher up Observatory Gully over rocky steps and steep snowfields (II). From the narrow section most teams go out right and up beneath steep rocks till overlooking the steep West Flank above Vanishing Gully. Cut back up left and follow the ridge to beneath the Little Tower, very exposed on all sides. The Little Tower usually requires three or four pitches of climbing, starting on the extreme left edge. After these pitches a short level section is reached before another pitch leads to the foot of the Great Tower. On the left side of the tower a very exposed and steeply banked snow ledge (The Eastern Traverse) is followed horizontally left past a slab corner and round an edge to beneath a huge fallen-block chimney. This chimney may be covered in snow. Ascend the chimney, steep walls and ledges to the top of the Great Tower with some difficulty. Follow the very narrow and exposed crest towards the Tower Gap, descending slightly. Climb down into the gap (tricky!) and either ascend the far wall or move left to belay beneath an icy slab. Ascend some difficult moves via slabs, ledges and chimneys until the angle eases. Climb the final section of the ridge to the plateau, moving right beneath a steep wall at the top.

Approaching Tower Gap in a very exposed position.
Climber: Martin Moran

N.B. It is possible to continue the Eastern Traverse by a delicate step further left from the foot of the chimney. This leads to steeply banked snowfields traversing to Tower Gully and avoids the difficulties higher up. This may be a good ploy for teams who are late and tired and wishing to avoid a night out. On reaching Tower Gully it is also possible to descend with care to the hut by a traverse beneath Gardyloo Buttress and on down Observatory Gully.

N.B. The first ascentionists overcame the Great Tower by taking the cliff on the west side (Western Traverse 70m III,4**). For fast parties on top form and blighted by queues on the Eastern Traverse this more difficult way may offer a chance to get in front and also lose your place in the line. Not for the faint-hearted!

CLIMBS ON THE DOUGLAS BOULDER

This large area of rock is the lower termination of Tower Ridge and lies immediately above the hut. It is triangular in shape and may provide good mixed climbing when higher routes are out of condition due to strong winds and avalanche potential.

Direct Route   215m   IV,4*
J.R. Marshall and party   1958
Start at the lowest rocks left of an obvious smooth slab. Follow a shallow groove (45m) to an open chimney. Follow this (60m) to a good ledge. Traverse right and climb steeply to the top of the Boulder.
N.B. Could be very difficult in lean conditions.

Down to the Wire   220m   V,6
B. Goodlad & J. Turner   23rd March 1993
Follow Direct Route to the base of the chimney (80m) and then the groove on the right (40m). Move up left, crossing Direct Route to follow the curving corner on the left (30m). Climb the corner to a spike and move to a slab on the right (30m). Overcome a leaning block then icy grooves to the top (40m).

North-West Face Route 215m   IV,5
A. Slater & G. Grassam   February 1980

Seen from the C.I.C. Hut three chimneys form an inverted 'N' on the Douglas Boulder. This route follows the central chimney. Gain the chimney which is followed until 6m below a chockstone. Traverse slabs to a rib on the right and climb up to regain the top of the chimney. Follow snow ramps and grooves to the S.W. Ridge.

Left-Hand Chimney   215m   IV,4
R. Carrington and J.R. Marshall   February 1972
This route climbs the left-hand chimney (see previous route). Start from the left and traverse over snow from the lowest rocks. Gain the chimney by a short vertical wall and follow it with sustained difficulties to the top.

Gutless   180m   IV,5
P. McKenna and D. Sanderson   March 1979
Some 30m left of the South-West Ridge (left of West Gully) a corner can be seen (Cutlass - summer VS). Left of that corner is a prominent chimney which is climbed to a rightward sloping ledge (90m). Climb ledge to edge of the buttress and on to the top of the Boulder.

Western Grooves   195m   IV,5
T. Anderson & G.E. Little   8th April 1979
Start in the snow bay left of Cutlass and trend up left to the foot of a shallow groove (45m). Climb the corner-groove for two pitches to a flake. Go left round a rib and climb a ramp to belay below a semi-detached flake. Follow the groove above and a right-trending ramp towards the S.W. Ridge.

Cutlass   145m   VI,7*
A. Clarke & J. Main   24th March 1989
The clean-cut corner 30m left of the S.W. Ridge. Climb the corner, a chimney and a cracked wall to reach the S.W. Ridge.

South West Ridge   180m   III*
J.Y. McDonald and H.W. Turnbull   March 1934
Follow the crest of the ridge bounding the left side of Douglas Gap Gully West.

Douglas Gap West Gully   180m   I**

A straightforward ascent on steep snow, better scenery than the East Gully. A good low level outing is the combination of Douglas Gap West Gully, followed by the descent of the Douglas Gap East Gully.

CLIMBS FROM COIRE NA CISTE

From the C.I.C. Hut there are several approach routes into Coire na Ciste. The time taken to the higher routes can be as much as an hour. 200m south-west of the C.I.C. Hut is a steep rocky bluff with deep gorges on its left and right-hand sides. The left-hand gorge has been the scene of some fatal avalanche accidents over the years. Debris appears from the Garadh Buttress area and as far afield as No.2 Gully and Comb Gully! When approaching routes on the left (south) side of the corrie it is best to skirt this gorge on the right where it looks easiest and traverse in high above the gorge beneath Garadh Buttress. Initial difficulties soon ease. Vanishing Gully area can be approached by moving in from close beneath the Douglas Boulder, well above the gorge on its left. The most straightforward approach into Coire na Ciste is by the slopes right (N.W.) of the right-hand gorge mentioned above, or the gorge itself if it has a good banking of snow.

The major features of Coire na Ciste when seen from the hut are from left to right: Tower Ridge and Secondary Tower Ridge, Garadh Gully and Buttress (Garadh na Ciste) the thin gullies of No.2 and Comb (exits unseen), the triangle of Comb Buttress, the obvious gap of No.3 Gully (lowest point on the skyline), Creag Coire na Ciste, the Trident Buttress area and low down to the left of No.5 Gully is Moonlight Gully Buttress.

Fawlty Towers   155m   II
T. McAulay and N. Muir   2nd April 1980
Take the first icefall right of Douglas Gap West Gully and follow slightly rightwards to the first narrow crest of Tower Ridge.

1934 Route   185m   II/III**
J.Y. MacDonald and H.W. Turnbull   March 1934

TOWER RIDGE WEST FLANK

1. DOUGLAS GAP GULLY WEST
2. 1934 ROUTE
3. VANISHING GULLY
4. ITALIAN CLIMB
5. THE CHUTE
6. GARADH GULLY
7. BROAD GULLY
8. PINNACLE BUTTRESS OF TOWER
9. PINNACLE BUTTRESS DIRECT
10. PINNACLE BUTTRESS
11. GLOVER'S CHIMNEY
12. THE WHITE LINE
13. RAEBURN'S EASY ROUTE
14. LE PANTHERE ROSE

NO.2 GULLY

TOWER GAP

GREAT TOWER

GARADH BUTTRESS

DOUGLAS GAP

West Flank of Tower Ridge area

Start 45m right of Douglas Gap West Gully, further right again than Fawlty Towers. Climb via grooves and snow bays until a shallow gully can be gained via icy slabs on the right. This gully leads to the snow shelf above the hard pitches of Vanishing Gully and leads with one short icy section to Tower Ridge below the Little Tower. An alternative for a short day is to climb direct to Tower Ridge instead of taking the shallow gully up right, followed by a fairly easy descent into Observatory Gully on the east side. A good low grade low level outing.

Running Hot   120m   V,5
M. Duff, J. Tinker & R. Nowack   8th February 1986
Start just left of Vanishing Gully and climb slabs towards a leftwards traverse which is taken for a short way until it is possible to climb another slab to a recess beneath a roof. Overcome the roof on the right and go diagonally left to a corner and short wall which gains a stance in a corner. Go right to a groove and descend 3m, then right to another groove which is climbed to a spike. Exit left and on to the top.

Vanishing Gully   200m   V,5***
R. Marshall and G. Tiso   15th January 1961
Start at an icefall about 100m right of Douglas Gap West Gully and climb to a cave with good belays. Climb out of the cave on very steep ice and continue until easier ground leads right to Tower Ridge. It is quicker to descend the ridge from this point rather than carry on up.
N.B. The cave belay is often blocked out by ice. After the second hard pitch (it is possible to reach the large snowfield in two fifty metre run-outs) a traverse left leads to the top of a shallow gully (1934 Route) which can be down-climbed or abseiled. This is a good alternative if short on time or good weather.

Pirate   150m   IV,4
M. Duff & A. Nisbet   3rd January 1986
20m right of Vanishing Gully. Move easily up left on a snow ramp, over a wall and into a small left-facing corner (45m). Slabs left of the

corner to a steep wall bounded on the right by a large corner. Go right beneath the corner and ascend the rib right of second corner, then slant left into a vertical corner (45m). Follow the corner then right into a shallow chimney (30m) and grooves to the crest of Secondary Tower Ridge (45m).

Fish Eye Chimney   150m   V,5
N. Holmes & D. Lampard   January 1987
Climbs an obvious parallel-sided slot just right of Pirate. Start just left of 1931 Route and traverse on mixed ground awkwardly up left to the base of the chimney. Climb the chimney (50m) and a large groove to the crest of Secondary Tower Ridge.

1931 Route   125m   III
G. Wallace & R. Shaw   21st January 1961
Start in a bay 150m right of Douglas Gap West Gully formed by a steep buttress from which two chimneys lead to the crest of Secondary Tower Ridge. Climb the chimney for three short pitches to the large snowfield of 1934 Route which is followed either up or down.

Rogue's Rib   220m   IV,4
I.S. Clough & G. Grandison   2nd January 1960
Takes the two-tier buttress which projects from Tower Ridge left of Italian Climb. Start up Italian Climb (original line) then by cracks and grooves to the top of the buttress.

The Italian Climb   180m   III*
J. Marshall, A. MacCorquodale and G. Ritchie   January 1958
Continuing along beneath the west side of Tower Ridge one comes to a deep gully bounded on the left by a prominent two-tier rib. Climb the gully; after a starting pitch easy snow leads to another pitch giving access to a huge recess. Traverse right and ascend an easy snow slope (frequent avalanche danger) to Tower Ridge.

Italian Climb - Right-Hand   65m   IV,4***
S. Belk and I. Fulton   February 1973
A popular variation which takes the obvious icefall above the start

of the first pitch and parallel and right of the main gully. The icefall is long and a poor belay must be taken before the upper snow slope is reached.

Bydand 150m V,5*
M. Duff, M. Aldridge & J. Woods 31st January 1986
Climb two steep icy chimneys and a sharply defined curving groove right of Italian Climb.

The Chute 230m V,4**
J.R. Marshall, R.N. Campbell and R. Holt February 1965
About 40m right of Italian Climb this route does not often come into condition, but when it does an excellent route is the result. Climb by an extremely steep entry pitch, left then right into a groove which is followed to a ledge (45m) which leads across a steep wall into a small gully (35m). Traverse up right to beneath a steep ice wall (35m). Climb the ice (25m) and the gully beyond (65m) to the base of a steep buttress. Move easily right into Broad Gully, which can be descended to the corrie or ascended to Tower Ridge.

Garadh Gully 95m II/III or I !!
I. Clough and M. Burke 16th February 1958
Starts just above and right of Italian Climb and separates the steep little buttress of Garadh na Ciste from Tower Ridge. Can be difficult early in the season, but easy later on. (Easily seen from C.I.C. Hut.)

Garadh Buttress 95m III
N. Muir and G. Whitten February 1970
Climb the buttress right of Garadh Gully by a line of snow and ice ramps up its centre.

Broad Gully 95m II
I.S. Clough and M. Burke 16th February 1958
From the top of Garadh Gully follow the line of least resistance up leftwards skirting the large buttress above (Pinnacle Buttress) to the crest of Tower Ridge.

To the right of the Garadh and above the exit of the gorge

approach, a long snow slope tapers up between the flanks of Tower Ridge and the prominent conical buttress of The Comb, to terminate as No.2 Gully. This slope is the approach for the next climbs.

Pinnacle Buttress of the Tower   250m   III,4*
D.J. Bennett and A. Tait   17th November 1957
Starting from the top of Garadh na Ciste, Broad Gully is followed to the left for about 50m before traversing right along a ledge above overhanging rocks and beneath the steep crest of the buttress. Beyond the crest the rocks are more broken, and the climb now follows a series of snow grooves in the right flank until it is possible to move leftwards to the top of the buttress. Follow a ridge to the foot of the Great Tower and traverse right until a line of chimneys can be followed to the top of it.

Pinnacle Buttress Direct   200m   V,5**
R. Clothier & G. Armstrong   March 1989
The start of this route may be independent, but thereafter it could have much in common with either the previous or the next route. Start midway between Glover's Chimney and Broad Gully in a snow bay and follow a break up on the right side. Climb a ramp then an icy wall followed by a groove line to the Great Tower.

Pinnacle Buttress   200m   IV,4
R. Carrington and B. Hall   March 1976
Start as for Glover's Chimney and climb the icefall to the left of that route to easier ground on the left of the Chimney. Take either of the chimneys above and continue to the top of the Great Tower.

Glover's Chimney   200m   III,4***
G.G. MacPhee, G.C. Williams and D. Henderson   17th March 1935
Starts above Garadh na Ciste and follows a long couloir leading to a chimney below the Tower Gap. The entry is made by an icefall, often over 35m high and very steep, usually climbed from left to right. The final chimney is the crux. The climb finishes in the Tower Gap. It is possible to descend into Observatory Gully and climb another route if time allows.

The White Line   275m   III**
M. Geddes and H. Gillespie   18th March 1971
Climb the icefall as for Glover's Chimney and continue to the right of the Chimney to a rightward slanting snow ledge. Climb an icefall to a snowfield. Above the snowfield climb a chimney and gully to finish at the top of Tower Ridge.
N.B. All but the initial icefall was originally climbed by T.E. Goodeve, C. Inglis-Clark and J.H.A. McIntyre on 28th December 1907, on an epic escape from Tower Ridge!

Raeburn's Easy Route   250m   II/III*
S.M.C. party   April 1920
The most obvious feature to the right of Glover's Chimney is the deep slit of No.2 Gully with The Comb to its right. To the left of No.2 Gully is No.2 Gully Buttress and to the left again an indefinite wall up which this route winds. Make a long traverse leftwards out of No.2 Gully, across a snow slope beneath The Cascade and aiming for a point where the crags peter out. Climb a low angled ice pitch then follow a snow shelf back right for a long way until a shallow gully gives access to the plateau midway between Tower Ridge and No.2 Gully. It is possible to finish direct by going straight up after the initial icefall towards the exit of Tower Ridge (*III* R. Harvey & A. Meekin 1986*).

Beam Me Up Scotty   155m   III*
R.G. Reid & I. Crofton   March 1987
Start in a narrow snow bay above the beginning of the rightward traverse of Raeburn's Easy Route and follow a ramp line right before climbing icy grooves straight up.

No.2 Gully Buttress
To the left of No.2 Gully is an area known as No.2 Gully Buttress it extends as far as the icefall of Raeburn's Easy Route

The Cascade   50m   IV,5**
The obvious steep icefall below the right traverse of Raeburn's Easy Route.

The Upper Cascade   100m   IV,5
G. Perroux & J-P. Desterke   April 1991
Above The Cascade go up left to a steep curtain of ice. Climb vertically at first then more easily to the top.

Le Panthere Rose   50m   VI,6*
R. Clothier, B. Goodlad, G. Perroux & F. Bossier   11th April 1993
Above The Cascade climb the left hand column of steep ice in the headwall.

Rip Off   120m   IV,4*
P. Braithwaite and J. Lowe   March 1976
This route climbs the steep slabs and walls left of No.2 Gully Buttress. The most obvious feature is a diagonal fault running across the walls. Start right of this fault. Follow steep grooves and traverse left onto steep slabs after 45m. Climb the slabs with little protection for 75m!

Five Finger Discount   135m   IV,4**
M.G. Geddes and C. Higgins   4th February 1978
In the corner between the slabby face of Raeburn's Easy Route and No.2 Gully Buttress there is a deep groove, defining the left edge of the buttress. This groove is followed by Rip Off for 30m. Climb the groove till it bends left and steepens. Move left up an edge to a small gully and the finish.

Burrito's Groove   135m   IV,5**
M.G. Geddes and C. Higgins   8th April 1978
Between Five Finger Discount and No.2 Gully Buttress route is a distinct groove leading directly up the buttress, well seen from below Comb Buttress. Climb the groove passing an overhang on the left (45m). Often in condition.

 The slopes running up to all of the routes in this area of Ben Nevis are prone to serious avalanche risk after periods of strong winds and/or heavy snowfall.

No.2 Gully Buttress   120m   II/III**
J.R. Marshall, L.S. Lovat and A.H. Hendry   23rd March 1958
Immediately to the left of No.2 Gully. Steep snow and occasionally iced rocks lead to a shelf below a vertical upper wall. A short but difficult ice pitch on the left leads to easier ground.

No.2 Gully
Left of the obvious triangle of the Comb Buttress a narrow gully can be seen from the C.I.C. Hut (if weather allows) disappearing up left into steep rocks. Do not mistake Comb Gully for No.2 Gully. Comb Gully is very close on the left side of the buttress.

No.2 Gully   120m   I/II**
J. Collier, G. Hastings and W.C. Slingsby   Easter 1896
Hardest and possibly the most interesting of the easier gullies. Above the introductory slopes it becomes a deep slit. Generally a straightforward but steadily steepening slope, it can (especially early in the season) offer an ice pitch and the cornice is often quite difficult. Usually turned on the left.

Comb Gully Buttress   125m   IV,5
I.S. Clough and J.M. Alexander   8th January 1960
Immediately right of No.2 Gully is Comb Gully Buttress, with Comb Gully on its right side. Climb from just left of the lowest rocks to gain the central snowfield. Entry can also be made from No.2 Gully. Grooves on the left side of the snowfield lead up and right to the foot of a prominent curving chimney which is followed with a difficult exit to the left.
N.B. The chimney above is not often in condition and the following Variation is a better option and gives good climbing.

Variation   75m   IV,4**
I. Fulton and D. Gardner   3rd January 1971
After the grooves of Comb Gully Buttress on the left side of the buttress traverse left to ice column which is climbed to ice-filled grooves and easy ground.

Roaring Forties   140m   IV,5**
D. Lang & C. Stead   28th February 1988
Gain a belay right of the deep curving chimney of Comb Gully
Buttress (50m). Follow the deep groove 15m right of the chimney to
a ledge on the left (40m) and traverse left to the V-groove which is
climbed to the top (50m).

Comb Gully   125m   IV,4 **
F.G. Stangle, R. Morsley and P.A. Small   12th April 1938
The obvious gully running up the left side of The Comb. Easy snow
leads to the narrows from where a long pitch leads to a poor belay.
Above is a short, steep wall which often gives the crux. Easy ground
then leads to the top.

The Comb - Left Flank   100m   IV,4*
G.E. Little and R. Richardson   21st February 1981
Starts 20m above Hesperides Ledge. Follow ramp up right to belay
below obvious icefall. Climb the icefall and shallow gully to a belay
and then on to the top.

Hesperides Ledge   75m   III*
J.R. Marshall, J. Stenhouse and D. Haston   12th February 1959
Follows the lower 75m of Comb Gully and then a relatively easy but
highly spectacular steep curving shelf which leads rightwards
across the wall to the crest of The Comb.

The Good Groove   140m   V11,7**
S.M. Richardson & R.D. Everett   27th March 1993
A tiered ramp cuts the wall above Hesperides Ledge. Move left
along the second narrow ramp to a corner which is followed to a
belay at the end of a curving groove just right of Comb - Left Flank
(40m). Climb slabs right of the groove to a small stance below a steep
tapering corner (25m). Climb the corner with difficulty eventually
arriving at a platform (25m). Climb the wall above to an arête (50m).

Tower Face of Comb   215m   V,6***
R. Smith and R. Holt   January 1959

A difficult and sustained mixed climb which receives very few ascents. A large ledge splits the buttress diagonally at one-third height from left to right. From the bottom left end of this ledge move up to another ledge running parallel to the lower ledge (30m). Go right to the foot of an obvious groove (25m). Climb the groove, going left to easier climbing and the base of a steep wall (50m). Traverse right by walls and steep snow to the buttress crest. The easier ground above can be difficult in strong winds and deep snow. A variation start is possible *(50m V,5 R. Clothier & A. Shand 1987)* by following Comb Gully until it narrows and taking a groove right for 10m. Traverse right below the barrier to a leftward ramp which joins the original climb on pitch 3.

Don't Die of Ignorance   200m   VI,6
A. Cave & S. Yates   February 1987

Climbs the groove in the steep front face of Comb Buttress. From the diagonal fault line at one-third height climb up and around the prow on aid (large Friends) A2, then continue up the crack line on blades and R.Ps to a snow bay (30m). Ascend the corner at the back of the basin (45m) and continue up the chimney above to a cave, exiting left where the gully overhangs to gain the crest (45m) which is followed to the top.

Pigott's Route   245m   IV,5*
J. Marshall and R. Smith   12th February 1960

From the C.I.C. Hut an obvious large ramp/ledge can be seen cutting up from left to right across the bottom section of the triangle of Comb Buttress. Follow this ramp up right till beneath a chimney (35m left of Green Gully). Climb the chimney (hard) and traverse left into steep ice-filled grooves which are followed to the buttress crest.

Mercury   150m   IV,4**
M. Hind and J. Christie   26th January 1985

Ascends the right-most of four parallel grooves just left of Green Gully. Climb Green Gully for 10m and move left around a rib to belay beneath a chimney with a chockstone (20m, might be possible to climb direct). Climb up and traverse left (loose) past a small overhang to the main groove line on the left (30m crux). Continue up more easily to the crest of the buttress.

Green Gully   180m   IV,4***
H. Raeburn and E. Phildius   April 1906
A classic. The obvious gully running up the right side of Comb Buttress. The first pitch changes in character from steep ice to a Grade I/II snow slope depending on build-up. Good peg belays on the left wall after 45m. Above are normally two or three good ice pitches with belays on the right side of the gully wall. When the gully opens out to a steep snow slope near the top three exits present themselves. By easy snow to the right, a fine direct ice pitch (**) or a traverse left to the ridge. If the cornice presents a problem, one of these finishes should fix it!

No.3 Gully Buttress is the name given to the steep cliffs extending right from Green Gully to No.3 Gully. The very steep rocks at the left-hand side of the mouth of No.3 Gully have a snow bay on their left which gives access to the Original Route and others in this area. Alternative starts are described in the route details. Being high up the hill this area should provide good climbing, but be careful of the mean-looking cornices.

Venus   190m   V,5*
M. Duff and A. Nisbet   28th January 1982
Follows the arête which forms the right bank of Green Gully. At half-height it is possible to move into grooves on the right and then back onto the arête higher up. The stances are poor and a long rope (60m!) is recommended to avoid them. Avoiding moves are often possible to the right, making this a fairly artificial line. The top section of this climb is common with Aphrodite, described next.

Aphrodite   200m   IV,4**
M.G. Geddes and J.C. Higham   15th March 1971
Start up the same snow depression as Original Route (described later) and aim for the second snow ledge half-way up the face. Move

GREEN GULLY AND
NO.3 GULLY BUTTRESS

1. PIGOTT'S ROUTE
2. MERCURY
3. GREEN GULLY
4. VENUS
5. TRAMP
6. DIANA
7. APHRODITE

8. QUICKSTEP
9. NO.3 GULLY BUTTRESS
10. TWO STEP CORNER
11. THOMPSON'S ROUTE
12. GREMLINS
13. GARGOYLE WALL
14. WINTER CHIMNEY

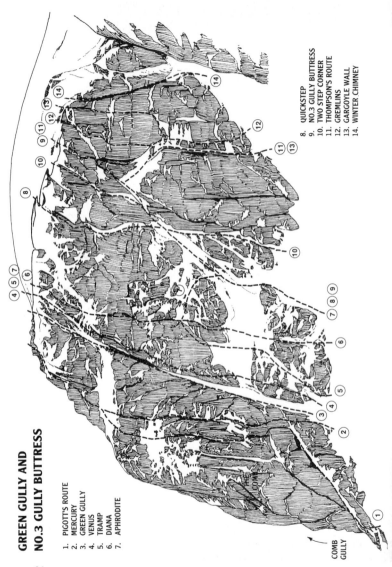

COMB GULLY

86

Pinnacle Buttress of Tower Ridge to Nº3 Gully Buttress, Ben Nevis

a long way left at the top over snowfields and ledges, then down with difficulty to the foot of an open groove. This groove is beside a rib right of Green Gully and is undercut by a large rock wall. Climb the groove and then the arête beside Green Gully, moving right at the top to a cornice which can be huge.

Tramp   180m   IV,4*
R. Clothier & C. Cartwright   January 1987
A direct approach to Aphrodite starting diagonally right up the icefall right of Green Gully. Cross the snow ledge above to beneath a left-facing chimney which is hidden from below. Ascend the chimney and the huge pedestal above and then a corner-crack which leads to the groove of Aphrodite.

Diana   195m   V,5*
M. Duff and J. Tinker   16th February 1985
Start further right than Tramp. Climb the icefall direct past a horizontal snow band to belay beneath a steep rock wall, (55m). On the left climb a groove/chimney past a roof/chockstone to another snow bank and huge block stance (45m). Follow corners to beneath a huge right-facing corner (30m). Up to the overlap and pull onto the right wall of the corner then straight up on steep thin ice to easier ground (45m). Follow snow to possible large cornice finish.

Quickstep   130m   V,5**
R. Townshend and T. Bray   26th March 1983
The huge leftward facing corner with steep slabs on its left, directly above the start of the Original Route. Climb the Original Route to the traverse ledge, then continue up to the foot of the corner. Steep ice on the left of the corner to belay at 45m. The final pitch leads to a conical basin above, which is often overhung by massive cornices which may be passable to the right by exposed and steep climbing.

No.3 Gully Buttress Original Route 125m   III***
L.S. Lovat and D.J. Bennet   18th February 1957
Climb up into the large snow bay below the prow of the buttress. From the top of the bay exit right to a platform, then follow grooves

leftwards to a steep corner finish or traverse up rightwards. The upper part of the route is magnificently exposed.

Two-Step Corner   130m   V,5***
D. Kirtley and D. Montgomery   March 1975
Starts 20m to the right of the Original Route and follows a corner to the traverse ledge of that route. Climb directly up the steep corner above to a difficult cornice exit.

Thompson's Route   120m   IV,4***
R. Marshall, J.R. Marshall and J. Stenhouse   December 1963
Immediately on the right of the very steep front face of the buttress at the bottom left of No.3 Gully, is a chimney. Follow this steeply and with interest to join the Original Route at the platform.

Gremlins   130m   VI,6
G. Perroux, C. Merlin, C. Biard & S. Hophster   March 1989
Climb the groove to the right and parallel with Thompson's Route to a steep icicle which is climbed, followed by a steep wall through overhangs. Then follow grooves to a ledge and the crack above direct to the plateau.

Gargoyle Wall   120m   IV,6*
R. Carrington & I. Nicholson   December 1977
From No.3 Gully a prominent head-shaped feature can be seen up on the left wall. Ascend the icy chimneys of Thompson's Route and traverse onto the Gargoyle. Climb the ridge above to a ledge then traverse right into a corner which is climbed to a stance below a steep wall (30m). Climb the steep crack above to a platform then go left to a chimney-crack which is climbed to a belay (30m). Climb the difficult chimney and then to the top (15m).

Winter Chimney   60m   IV,5*
D. Haston & D. Gray   March 1963
Lies in the back of the bay which defines the right side of Gargoyle Wall well up No.3 Gully.

CREAG COIRE NA CISTE

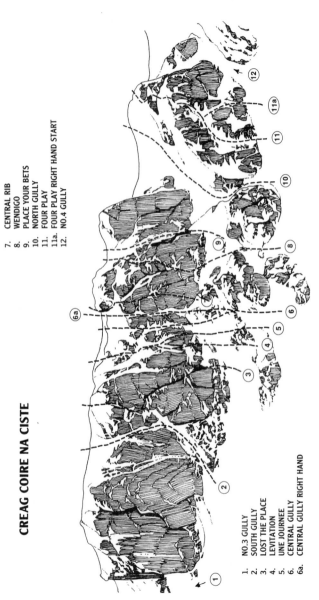

1. NO.3 GULLY
2. SOUTH GULLY
3. LOST THE PLACE
4. LEVITATION
5. UNE JOURNEE
6. CENTRAL GULLY
6a. CENTRAL GULLY RIGHT HAND

7. CENTRAL RIB
8. WENDIGO
9. PLACE YOUR BETS
10. NORTH GULLY
11. FOUR PLAY
11a. FOUR PLAY RIGHT HAND START
12. NO.4 GULLY

No.3 Gully 150m I***

The lowest point in the skyline looking S.W. from the C.I.C. Hut.
First ascent dates back to pre-1870. The angle of the approach slope
gradually increases as it rises from the basin of Coire na Ciste and
by the time it narrows to a gully proper, it is quite steep. No pitches
but the final section is divided by a pinnacle rib. The exit will be
dictated by the cornice.

South Gully, Creag Coire na Ciste 125m III
G.G. MacPhee 10th April 1936

Starts high up on the left-hand side of Creag Coire na Ciste and just
below No.3 Gully proper. Use an obvious ramp slanting diagonally
to the right. This leads to an ice pitch which gives entry to a final
steep funnel. Cornice is often difficult.

Lost the Place 140m IV,4
C. Cartwright & R. Clothier 17th December 1988

Follow a groove starting just left of Central Gully until it overlooks
South Gully then traverse right to a chossy chimney leading to the
cornice.

Une Journee Ordinaire dans un Enfer Quotidien 105m
VI,6*
G. Perroux, F. Bossier & J. Douay 15th April 1993

Ascend Central Gully for 10m then go left to the foot of another
icefall which is climbed with an exit left and continuation to belay
on the left (45m). Continue up snow and more ice to the cornice
which can be huge and may require a long traverse left with some
tunnelling!

Levitation 115m VI,6**
D. Cuthbertson & J. George 20th April 1993

Initially difficult mixed climbing followed by steep ice. Climb
Central Gully for 10m and traverse left (crux) beneath an overlap to
a steep icicle on the prow which is climbed (30m), followed by easier
snow to belay below the steep upper section (35m). Climb ice then
traverse left as in previous route.

Central Gully   125m   III**
I. Clough and J.M. Alexander   27th January 1959
Starting from the lowest part of the crag, snow slopes are followed
to the left of a rocky rib to reach the left-hand of two parallel ice
chimneys which cleave the steep central wall. This is climbed for
40m before crossing to the right-hand gully which leads into the
final corniced funnel.

Central Gully - Right-Hand   125m   IV,4***
I. MacEacheran and J. Knight
The right-hand chimney gives a fine long pitch. An independent
start can be made by climbing the rightward slanting icefall to the
left of North Gully then traversing left to the foot of the chimney.

Central Rib   120m   III,4*
R.N. Campbell & J.R. Marshall   March 1970
Start at the lowest point of the cliff and climb steeply up the edge
overlooking Central Gully Right-Hand to finish on a ledge running
round left under the final tower.

Wendigo   110m   IV,4 **
T.W. Patey & J. Brown   24th February 1963
Start right of Central Rib beneath a steep icefall and go steeply up
right to a large ledge. Climb mixed ground above to the cornice.

Place Your Bets   100m   V,6+
J. Blyth, J. Briel, G. Perroux, D. Colin   12th April 1994
An overhanging icefall to the right of Wendigo which seldom forms.

North Gully   110m   II
J.Y. MacDonald and H.W. Turnbull   24th March 1934
The right-hand and most obvious of the three gullies on this cliff,
starts to the left of No.4 Gully. The lower section of the gully almost
always holds an ice pitch but its length may vary from 3m to 30m.
The narrow lower section leads to a wide easier angled slope which
is followed obliquely rightwards to the cornice. Beware of avalanche
danger on the final slopes. A left fork finish is possible *(35m III, D.
Bathgate, J. Knight, A. McKeith February 1964)* up an ice groove at the

Coire Na Ciste, Ben Nevis

back of a steep scoop above the upper snow basin.

Four Play   110m   IV,4
J. Raitt & D. Gibson   13th February 1993
A thin V-groove between North Gully and No.4 Gully. Start just left
of where No.4 Gully widens.

No.4 Gully   150m   I
The easiest winter route on Ben Nevis and the best descent on the
North Face. It curls gently round to the right between the cliffs of
Creag Coire na Ciste and the South Trident Buttress. Its exit is very
wide so that, even given a heavy build-up of cornice, it should be
possible to find an easy weakness. This route cannot be seen from
the C.I.C. Hut.

The area which extends from No.4 Gully on the left to No.5
Gully on the right contains the **Trident Buttress group (South,
Central and North)** whose crests can be seen cutting the skyline.
The following routes are located on these rocks, starting from
Lochan na Ciste (GR 162718).

No.4 Gully Buttress   100m   II*
J.H.B. Bell   1st January 1929
The broken area to the right of the lower reaches of No.4 Gully and
left of South Trident Buttress.

South Flank Route   150m   IV,4*
A. Kimber, N. Hicking & C. Collin   29th March 1994
To the left of the steep rocks of the middle tier of South Trident
Buttress overlooking the approach to No.4 Gully are some steep ice
smears. Follow the steepest of these and snow slopes and chimneys
above to the flat section on the crest of South Trident Buttress whose
fine narrow shattered arête is followed to the top.

Rien ne va Plus   50m   V5
G. Perroux & J. Blyth   10th April 1994
An icefall which sometimes forms on the left side of the lowest rocks
of South Trident Buttress.

TRIDENT BUTTRESSES

1. RIEN NEVA PLUS
2. EASTERN BLOCK
3. JOYFUL CHIMNEYS
4. CENTRAL GULLY
5. JUBILATION
6. MEGE REVE
7. JUBILEE CLIMB
8. MEGA ROUTE X
9. NEPTUNE GULLY
10. MOONLIGHT GULLY
11. DIAGONAL ROUTE

Eastern Block 125m VI,6
G. Livingston & M. Charlton January 1987
A hard mixed climb which starts about 30m right of the lowest rocks
of South Trident Butresss at a steep wall (30m). Go left of the steep
chimney, then trend left to a belay ledge (25m). Traverse the ledge
to some stacked blocks and climb the bulging wall above to another
ledge (15m) and continue more easily to the right end of a large
snowfield from where it is possible to descend leftwards.

The Groove Climb 80m V,6*
J. Main & A. Clarke 22nd December 1992
Under the middle tier is a deep chimney-groove which is climbed
to a deep cave (30m). From the cave an awkward exit is made to a
belay (10m). Go left by an icy ramp to the top from where it is
possible to descend left.

The Clanger 90m IV,5**
J.R. Marshall, R. Marshall & R.N. Campbell March 1967
Climb the chimney groove at the back of the corner near the right
end of the middle tier to a steep cave pitch (35m). Exit the cave by
a through-route on the right wall leading behind a large flake onto
the buttress crest. Easier to the top. A route for people of slight
stature!?

Pinnacle Arête 150m IV,4**
R.H. Sellars & J. Smith 1st February 1959
Start from the right end of the snow ledge (middle ledge) and climb
a series of grooves just right of the crest.

Joyful Chimneys 180m III
R. Campbell, J.R. Marshall February 1971
A discontinuous line of chimneys can be seen on the flank of South
Trident Buttress facing the C.I.C. Hut. Starts 50m left and downhill
of Central Gully (described next). These chimneys are either climbed

Shot in the dark (IV), Ben Nevis. Climber: Mark Seaton

or avoided on their flanks, depending on conditions. The crest of South Trident Buttress is gained by a series of grooves above the chimneys.

Central Gully   240m   III
H. Raeburn and Mr & Mrs C. Inglis-Clark   April 1904
Immediately above (west) of the small lochans (Lochan Coire na Ciste) and right of the steep rocks of South Trident Buttress. This gully can fill up almost completely. Often a steep ice column is found baring the way. Either pass it by mixed ground up to the left (as on the first ascent) or climb direct *(30m III,4 L.S. Lovat & K. Bryan 11th March 1956)*. Above a variety of routes lead to the top avoiding difficulties as necessary.

Mega Rêve   60m   V,5
G. Perroux, J.P. Destercke, C. Deu, P. Gratadour, F. Domanget   4th April 1994
Climb narrow chimney to the left of Jubilee Climb snow slope. A short steep icefall is followed by the central of three vertical icefalls.

Jubilee Climb   240m   II
G.G. MacPhee, G.C. Williams and D. Henderson   May 1935
In the lower part of Central Gully is a rightward leading branch which is followed on snow and small ice pitches to easy ground and a choice of routes to the top.

Jubilation   240m   IV,4*
R. Marshall, J.R. Marshall and J. Stenhouse   December 1963
Follow Jubilee Climb for about 75m. Traverse left into a chimney and climb it on steep ice to a snow bay. Move left into a second chimney and follow this until it eases. A choice of routes lead over easier ground to the top.

Climbers John Taylor and Tom Whittaker on the first pitch of Waterfall Gully (III/IV), Ben Nevis

Mega Route X   70m   VI,6***
J. Murphy & A. Cain   18th December 1982
One of the steeper ice climbs on Ben Nevis which takes the lowest section of Central Trident Buttress 50m right of Jubilee Climb. A good belay at 40m on the left below an overhang.

Neptune Gully   160m   Grade III
A.J. Bennet and J. Clarkson   February 1956
This S-shaped gully splits the crest of the North Trident (right-hand) Buttress. It has an indefinite entry pitch 10m to the left of the upper section of Moonlight Gully (described below) from the large flat ledge. Climb first on the right and enter the gully higher up which is followed turning ice pitches on the left to a large platform overlooking No.5 Gully. Ascend an easy ridge and slopes above to the plateau.

North Trident Buttress   200m   III**
J. Maclay, H. Raeburn, C.W. Walker & H. Walker   1904
Climbs the buttress on the left of Moonlight Gully. The line is variable depending on conditions and the final tower is not climbed.

Central Rib Direct   150m   IV
P. Macdonald & A. McKeith   18th February 1967
Gained from the upper section of Moonlight Gully this climb ascends the middle of three distinct narrow ribs on the right side of North Trident Buttress. A lot of aid was used on the right arête of the final tower.

At the bottom of No.5 Gully on the left is Moonlight Gully Buttress which is split at two-thirds height by a very large (almost flat) ledge. At such a low altitude the climbs will not be in good condition so often, but offer alternatives when the weather high up is bad.

Moonlight Gully   150m   I/II
W. Inglis-Clark and T. Gibson   January 1908
This gully is on the immediate left of Moonlight Gully Buttress and provides a steep and narrow snow climb which ends in the upper area of No.5 Gully.

Diagonal Route   150m   II/III*
D. Hawthorn, C. MacLean and A. Paul   17th December 1983
Start at the foot of Moonlight Gully. Traverse up right to a broad
ledge and continue by the left-hand chimney above to the big ledge.
Climb the upper tier by the continuation of the chimney.

Right-Hand Chimney   135m   III,4**
D. Hawthorn, C. MacLean and A. Paul   17th December 1983
Two chimneys split the front face of the buttress. The right-hand one
is better defined and is climbed direct and its continuation followed
on the second tier above the big ledge, sustained.

Gaslight   90m   IV,4
M. Duff & R. Parsley   8th February 1989
Climb to the right of Right-Hand Chimney to a large roof then enter
Right-Hand Chimney. Above the roof gain the right edge of the
buttress which is followed to the top.

Phosphorescent Grooves   175m   III,4*
K.V. Crocket, A. Walker and R.T. Richardson   22nd December 1985
A traverse line up the face overlooking No.5 Gully. Start just left of
the gully entrance and climb easily to a large ledge. Up a steep wall
and right to belay on a large ledge by a slab corner. Climb the corner
to a belay and go right into an awkward 5m chimney, which is
climbed to another belay. Descend a little then up to the large ledge
above.

No.5 Gully   460m   I*
Collie and party   April 1895
Obvious from the C.I.C. Hut. Prone to very large avalanches. Lies
between the Trident Buttresses and the Great Buttress of Carn
Dearg and commences below and well to the right of the main basin
of Coire na Ciste. It is a straightforward snow climb. Above a small
pitch the gully narrows, and then opens into a huge funnel. The
normal route keeps to the right, to exit near the top of Carn Dearg
N.W. depending on the cornice.

Ledge Route   450m   II***

The best on the mountain at this grade. A very interesting excursion. Starts up No.5 Gully but leaves it by a rightwards rising ramp shortly after it becomes a gully proper. The ramp leads out above the top of The Curtain onto a broad, almost horizontal ledge which fades out to the right. Before the ledge narrows, leave it by a leftward slanting gully which comes out onto a broad sloping snow shelf. This shelf gives an easier but less interesting start; it comes out of No.5 Gully and slants easily up to the right to a large platform at the summit of the Great Buttress of Carn Dearg. A large pinnacle block, a useful landmark, is passed just before rounding the corner to reach the platform. The route now follows the ridge and is in places very narrow. A further connecting ridge leads on up to the summit of Carn Dearg N.W. In good weather this route gives a more interesting, if slower, descent than the gullies.

In Descent

The ridge should be followed down to the top of Carn Dearg Buttress and then the broad highest shelf (marked by the pinnacle block at the start) can be followed easily into No.5 Gully. Instead of descending the gully (which may have a small pitch in it), continue to the far side where a similar broad shelf leads gradually down from the large ledge at the top of Moonlight Gully Buttress, towards Lochan na Ciste. This descent passage also provides a good approach if avalanches are possible in No.5 Gully.

CARN DEARG BUTTRESS

The Great Buttress of Carn Dearg lies to the right of No.5 Gully and contains some of the most difficult winter climbs in Scotland. On the steep tier of rocks 100m below the buttress a number of icefalls may form, providing good practice at a variety of grades.

The Curtain Rail   80m   IV,4*

D.F. Land, R.T. Richardson and C. Stead   31st January 1988 (first recorded ascent!)

Follows the grooves left of and parallel to The Curtain (described next) and can provide an interesting alternative to that overcrowded climb.

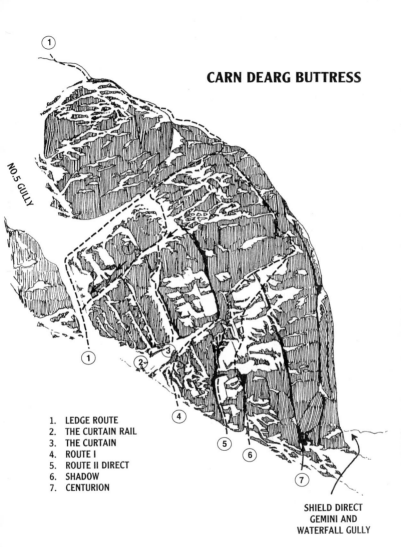

CARN DEARG BUTTRESS

NO.5 GULLY

1. LEDGE ROUTE
2. THE CURTAIN RAIL
3. THE CURTAIN
4. ROUTE I
5. ROUTE II DIRECT
6. SHADOW
7. CENTURION

SHIELD DIRECT
GEMINI AND
WATERFALL GULLY

101

The Curtain   110m   IV,5***
J. Knight and D. Bathgate   February 1965
Climbed more times than any other ice route in Britain.

On the left side of Carn Dearg Buttress immediately right of No.5 Gully, and a definite candidate for a multiple pile-up. One day a climber will fall from the top pitch and wipe out all the ropes below. Absurd tactics have been seen on this route, with two separate parties climbing in parallel on all of the three pitches. If you value your life, try and climb the route on a quiet day which is not often possible. For people staying in the hut, they should be able to ascend the route either before or after the hordes have arrived or descended!

A 50m rope is useful to gain the cave belay on the first pitch and to reach the rocks after the last pitch. Climb the long slab to a belay on the right 45m. Zig-zag up the next pitch to belay on the left wall. Traverse right and climb the final steep ice wall and slab.
N.B. If the belayer lets the ropes hang down the second pitch, they can easily get caught under the icicle fringe. Descent is made into No.5 Gully by a steep snow slope on the left after the final difficulties.

P.M.   110m   V,6
B. Hall & A. Rouse   10th February 1986
From the foot of The Curtain an obvious ledge runs right above very steep ground to a large deep chimney (Route I, described next) after approximately 60m. This line follows a corner (turf) to the left of the chimney for two pitches then crosses the chimney for an exciting finish on the right.
N.B. Climbed in good conditions on the first ascent, this route may vary in difficulty considerable. Also it appears that this route was climbed in 1985 by Mal Duff and J. Tinker using the direct start of Route II, following the turf line mentioned on P.M. and finishing up Route I, instead of crossing that climb as did Hall/Rouse. They called their climb **Sod's Law** *300m V,6*.

Route I   175m   V,6**
D. Knowles and D. Wilson   1972
An obvious ledge runs right from the foot of The Curtain. After about 60m it arrives at the bottom of a large obvious chimney. This

chimney gives the top half of the climb and can be very hard. It is possible to take a more direct start by climbing the minor buttress below and to the right of The Curtain and traversing the ledge mentioned above to the foot of the chimney section.

Route I Direct   80m   VI,6***   (Grade for the combined route)

D. Cuthbertson & J. Sylvester   March 1984
Start as for Route II Direct but transfer into left-hand crack after approximately 10m. Climb the corner and then move left across the wall to gain the rib which leads more easily to the ledge beneath the chimney

Route II   150m   V,6**
M. Geddes and A. Rouse   12th February 1978
Climb the first pitch of the chimney of Route I (20m). Then follow an upward diagonal line across the slabs, beneath the overhangs, rightwards to a groove line at the far edge of the buttress. Follow this groove line up the crest to easy ground. A superb climb in an exciting situation, not often in condition. Three pegs were used for tension on the first ascent.

Route II Direct   275m   VI,6***
G. Smith and I. Sykes   15th February 1978
Starts in a deep corner at the lowest point of rocks right of Route I Direct start. Climb the corner and traverse left beneath an overhang. Climb up to a large block and climb a groove above it. Traverse right round an arête to a ledge and climb bulge above to the traverse ledge. Follow the Geddes/Rouse route to the top. Combined with the original Route II climb (Geddes/Rouse), the Direct provides a high quality route of considerable difficulty when in condition.

Ring The Alarm   270m   VI,5***
M. Duff & J. Tinker   1st February 1986
Start just right of the direct start to Route II and climb the crack (45m). Follow Route II for 10m and traverse across The Shadow to a stance on the slab edge (30m). Stay calm whilst traversing the lip

of the slab to a groove which is climbed over an overlap to a stance (45m). Climb ice (The Weep) above to reach Route II (30m) which is followed to the top (120m).

Overload Finish   155m   VI,6
R. Clothier & D. Heselden   27th February 1988
From the top of pitch three climb the icefall and slab, then go right to Centurion (45m). Overcome the step above and go horizontally right above the overlap to the edge of the buttress (30m). Up the groove to Route II (20m) which is followed to the top (60m).

The Shadow   245m   VII,6**
P. Braithwaite and D. Pearce   March 1979
Starts 10m right of Route II Direct. Follow a crack-line and groove to belay (20m). Traverse right, continuing to an obvious line of overhangs beneath the traverse line of Route II. Continue this traverse right to the junction with Centurion, which is gained with difficulty (40m). Continue across Centurion and up right to below large overhang (20m). Climb exposed broken crack-line through right side of overhangs to snowy recess on arête (15m). Climb overhanging groove until a difficult move left can be made onto icy rib. Climb rib with difficulty, then move slightly left to join Sassenach and follow grooves above to finish.

Right-Hand Start   40m   VI,6*
R. Clothier & D. Heselden   February 1989
Climb a groove just right of the original route then overcome a block and make a difficult move left to gain the original climb.

Centurion   190m   VIII,8
Originally climbed solo using considerable aid over two days *(R. Milward 1975)*. Another ascent *(J. McKenzie & K. Spence 9th February 1986)* over two days used a bivouac and a rest point at the top of pitch two. The upper section has been avoided by finishing up Route II.

Start at the foot of the obvious corner in the centre of the face, climb the left wall to a belay (15m) then go right into the corner which is climbed to a belay in an overhung bay (35m). Go left to the edge and follow grooves until level with an overhang, then step right and up to a stance (25m). Go back into the corner then left across the wall to beneath an overhung crack. Ascend the arête to a stance (20m) then on up slabby grooves past a block to join Route II (40m).

Shield Direct   290m   VII,7***
M. Fowler and A. Saunders   March 1979
Originally, the first recorded Grade VI on the mountain, a soaring line of great difficulty. A long way right of the previous climbs the front face of Carn Dearg Buttress turns to form a vertical line of cliffs facing north. Waterfall Gully (described later) is an obvious feature to the right. On the vertical wall is a series of steep chimneys, which give the line of the route. Start in a steep icy groove (often blank), directly below the chimney line. Follow the groove to a stance at 24m. Climb steeply to a large ledge on the right at the foot of the chimney. Climb the difficult chimney to a cave (30m). Steep ice grooves lead to easier climbing at the top of the chimney flake (75m). Move left past a flake and bulges to trend right by easiest line to ledges (45m). Climb up right then left to easier ground, followed by an arête to the junction with Ledge Route.

Gemini   300m   VI,6***
A. Paul and D. Sanderson   23rd March 1979
Climb the first two pitches of Waterfall Gully (described next). Above on the left wall a series of rightward sloping ice ramps and steep ice smears sometimes form. These are followed to an enormous detached flake. Climb very steep ice on the wall left of the flake to a ledge and rightward sloping grooves. Move up and right to obvious twin grooves, either of which can be climbed to a broad ledge which is followed right. Climb up via iced slabs to easier ground.

A very steep direct start to the left of the first pitch of Waterfall Gully can be climbed, thus avoiding that route entirely. Combined with this start Gemini becomes one of the finest routes on Ben Nevis. *(A. McIntyre and A. Kimber 1st April 1979 V,6***)*

Gemini Left-Hand Finish   130m   V,5**
A. Fanshawe, A. Orgler, G.E. Little & R. Sailer   16th February 1988
From the ledge below the right-sloping grooves climb the groove on
the left to a ledge. Then go blindly (?) left and continue directly up
steep mixed ground (45m). Go right by an ice scoop then left along
a narrow ledge to a shallow cave (50m). Go left up into an open
slabby corner, then on to the top (35m).

Waterfall Gully   215m   IV,4*
D. Pipes, I. Clough, J. Alexander, R. Shaw and A. Flegg   8th January 1959
The obvious gully immediately right of Carn Dearg Buttress.

   After the first steep 45m the angle eases and leads with a
rightwards traverse after 150m to the large basin below the summit
buttresses. Keep to the left of this area and climb towards Ledge
Route. The first pitch of this route offers a good ice pitch followed
by abseil if time is short.

Waterfall Gully Direct Finish   VI,5**
D. Cuthbertson & C. Fraser   1984.
A direct finish to Waterfall Gully is possible by continuing straight
up where the gully swings right onto the ridge. Two pitches, the first
on ice up the big corner and the second (crux) is a short stiff pull over
the overhang. The crux is escapable.

Staircase Climb   215m   IV,5*
D. Haston & J. Stenhouse   February 1987
Starts 15m to the right of Waterfall Gully and climbs the higher of
two shelves sloping up rightwards. Around the corner a stepped
slab is climbed up right to beneath a clean-cut crack in a corner.
Climb the crack and a short wall to a platform. The chimney above
is climbed to easier ground and the buttress crest followed towards
a pinnacle which is turned on the left. Descend a little into Waterfall
Gully then move up to a steep slab leading to the col beyond the
pinnacle. Take the left-hand of two chimneys and continue up
towards the top of Carn Dearg Buttress.

Kellett's North Wall Route 200m   VII,7
M. Charlton & M. Burrows-Smith   1st February 1991
Starts left of The Shroud below a large flake with a deep chimney to
the right. Climb the chimney and exit by a window to continue to a
terrace (25m). Climb the corner to the left of an obvious crack to
reach another terrace (20m). Go 6m right then move up to a recess,
then go right to a steep groove which is climbed to a ledge (30m).
Move up left along the ledge and on up a steep turfy groove-line
(30m). Exit left into Waterfall Gully which is followed to the top
(95m).

The Shroud   200m   VII,6 *
A. Clarke & J. Main   2nd February 1993
In exceptional conditions an icy drape extends over the cliffs below
the hanging corrie left of Harrison's Climb Direct. Climb up to belay
on the right side of the icefall (50m). Continue to another belay on
a narrow ice ledge right of the free-hanging fang (25m). Follow the
fang to the upper ice wall and a semi-hanging belay on ice screws
(25m). Continue more easily above (100m) to the hanging snow
corrie

   High up above and to the right of Waterfall Gully is a large
hanging snow corrie. At its bottom lip an overhung icefall (The
Shroud) can often be seen from the approach to the C.I.C. Hut. To
the right of this icefall is an obvious snow/ice gully which gives the
start to some of the following routes. Access to these climbs can be
made from below the hut over the steep and rocky ground beneath
The Castle. Please be aware that many avalanche fatalities have
occurred in this area over the years. This approach is exposed to
these dangers for most of its length. A far safer approach is to ascend
from the hut to beneath the Carn Dearg Buttress and traverse below
it towards the climbs.

   Descent from the large hanging snow corrie is easiest by Ledge
Route, which is gained by ascending the steep slopes on the left side
of the corrie to the ridge above.

Harrison's Climb   275m   III**
C.G.M. Slesser & N. Tennent   1962
Down to the right of The Shroud is a deep chimney which separates

the main wall from an isolated buttress (Cousin's). Start 10m left of the chimney, climb up and right to enter the chimney and follow the ice corner above to the col. Go left to a thirty metre icefall which is climbed by its right edge followed by easier ground into the upper corrie from which a variety of exits can be made.

Harrison's Climb Direct   300m   IV,4***
K.V. Crocket & C. Gilmore   7th February 1976
This climb ascends the steep icy chimney direct then follows the original climb to the col. Traverse left to the icefall and climb a line up right to gain the edge overlooking Raeburn's Buttress. Continue for several pitches to the upper corrie and a variety of exits.
N.B. The hanging snow corrie often releases large avalanches, so be wary after strong winds and/or heavy snow falls.

North East Face Route (Cousin's Buttress Ordinary Route)
                        275m   III*
G.G. McPhee & G. F. Todd   April 1935
Follow the obvious snow/ice gully mentioned in the approach details previously, climbing one short ice pitch. Move left from below an ice-fall to the top of the buttress (Cousin's) mentioned in Harrison's Direct. Follow a ledge left and climb the right side of a large exposed ice-fall to the corrie above. A variety of exits are possible.

Boomer's Requiem   170m   V,5***
C. Higgins and D. MacArthur   February 1973
Above the approach gully on Raeburn's Buttress is an obvious icefall leading to a snow patch. Climb the icefall and up another ice pitch above the snow patch to beneath the summit gullies.

Continuation Wall   180m   IV,4
B. Dunn & D. Gardner   February 1977
Head up towards Boomer's Requiem and the bifurcation in the gully. Continue up the continuation chimney overcoming an ice step and heading up right to a steep snow gully which finishes on The Girdle Traverse Ledge. Either, traverse easily left and finish up one of the summit gullies (described later) or take the next route.

Baird's Buttress   90m   IV,4
B. Dunn & D. Gardner   February 1977
This route lies on the right edge of the upper corrie just left of Raeburn's Buttress and starts from a large ledge below a crack which splits the front of the buttress. Climb the crack and a steep wall above, then easier climbing to the top.

Raeburn's Buttress/Intermediate Gully   230m   IV,4**
W.D. Brooker and J.M. Taylor (by the buttress finish).   31st January 1959
R.H. Sellers and J. Smith (finishing by Intermediate Gully).   31st January 1959
G.G. MacPhee and party had previously made a first ascent of the gully in April 1938, but perhaps not under true winter conditions.
Raeburn's is the tall thin buttress above the left-hand corner of the Castle Corrie. It finishes as a slender tapering arête to the left of which is the prominent narrow Intermediate Gully. The start is the same as for North East Face Route; the gully leading up into the left-hand corner of the corrie. After about 65m an obvious chimney line on the right leads up to a cave (the impressive icefall of the left branch is Boomer's Requiem, described above) and then the route takes the right wall to reach the foot of Intermediate Gully. There is a cave exit at the top of the gully which is otherwise straightforward. The crest of Raeburn's Buttress proper is immediately to the right of the foot of the gully. It narrows to a sharp blade at the top but this may be turned by a corner on the right.

CARN DEARG SUMMIT GULLIES

These form a logical continuation to some of the previous climbs. They may also be reached by descending into the basin from high up on Ledge Route.

Colando Gully   105m   I
I. Clough, P.S. Nicholson & D. Pipes   8th April 1958
The left-hand gully. Straightforward.

Arch Buttress   185m   II/III
D. Pipes and A. Flegg   3rd January 1959

Between Arch and Colando gullies. After 45m on the crest, the route follows a groove on the right then easier climbing to some difficult chimneys.

Arch Gully   105m   I
I. Clough, P.S. Nicholson & D. Pipes   8th April 1958
The central gully marked by a huge block which forms the Arch at about half-height. Straightforward but steep.

Surprise Buttress   190m   III
I. Clough and B. Halpin   3rd January 1959
On the buttress to the right of Arch Gully, following the crest as closely as possible to a steep wall above the Arch block. A 33m rightwards traverse below this wall is followed by short awkward walls leading back slightly left to a small ledge about 10m above the traverse. A move downwards and to the right gives entry to a steep 35m corner which gives a strenuous final crux pitch.

Surprise Gully   185m   I/II
I. Clough, P.S. Nicholson & D. Pipes   12th April 1958
The shallow right-hand gully leads by broken rocks to a shoulder and to the top by an ice groove on the left.

CLIMBS FROM CASTLE CORRIE

On the approach up the Allt a'Mhuilinn the first main feature is the North Face of Castle Ridge up on the right, to its left is Castle Ridge. The area to the left of Castle Ridge is known as Castle Corrie and is only seen fully from a point approximately half a kilometre down hill of the hut. The main features are the North and South Castle Gullies which are separated by The Castle at their top, and join at their foot into a steep rocky icefall/gully descending towards the Half Way Lochan approach path. The approaches to the climbs and hazards involved are the same as for the routes to the right of Carn Dearg Buttress.

Compression Crack   130m   V,5*
M. Hind and C. Rice   9th February 1985

CASTLE CORRIE AREA

1. ROUTE II DIRECT
2. CENTURION
3. THE SHIELD DIRECT
4. GEMINI
5. WATERFALL GULLY
6. STAIRCASE CLIMB
7. THE SHROUD

8. HARRISONS DIRECT
9. BOOMER'S REQUIEM
10. BAIRD'S BUTTRESS
11. RAEBURN'S BUTTRESS
12. COMPRESSION CRACK
13. SOUTH CASTLE GULLY

14. THE CASTLE
15. NORTH CASTLE GULLY
16. CASTLE RIDGE
17. THE MOAT
18. THE SERPENT

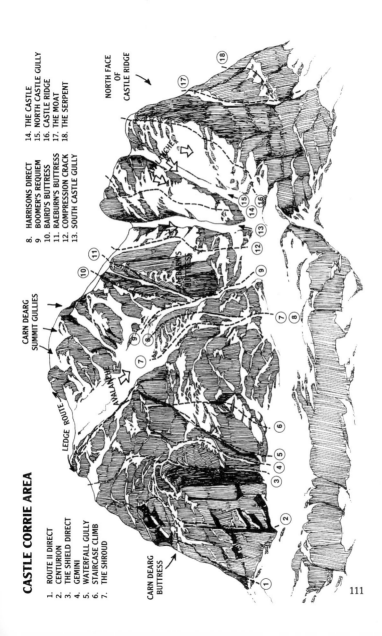

111

On the steep wall left of South Castle Gully and below Raeburn's Arête a series of imposing ice smears can often be seen. Climb this ice and traverse a long way right to reach iced cracks. Follow the corner above vertically for 15m and a further 20m to easy ground.

Winter Chimneys   145m   IV,4
I.S. Clough and R. Sefton   28th January 1960
Although little is known about this route it is given as a possible landmark for the previous climb. Go beyond Compression Crack for about 30m to a deep chimney topped by a huge capstone. The capstone was avoided by pegging on the right wall on the first ascent.

CASTLE GULLIES

These two climbs can be anything from straightforward snow ascents, to awkward chockstone-filled trenches depending on the amount of snow. They are also very prone to avalanches after strong winds and/or snowfall.

South Castle Gully   230m   I/II*
W. Brunskill, W.W. King and W.W. Naismith   1st April 1896
The long gully between Raeburn's Buttress and The Castle. Normally an easy snow climb. One small pitch may be particularly difficult early in the season; climbed by a gangway on the left wall. Near the top of the left wall of the gully is an obvious icefall **Plum Duff** 60m IV,4 *(D. Hawthorn & J. Murphy February 1984).*

The Castle   230m   II/III*
W. Brown, J. MacLay, W.W. Naismith and G. Thomson   April 1896
In summer an awkward bulging little wall guards the base. This may be hard in winter but more probably it will be entirely obliterated by an avalanche cone. the route then goes straight up. The upper rocks are climbed by means of a gully, slabs, a chimney and a further shallow gully all in the centre of the buttress, to beneath the final very steep wall. The route now goes up to the right over snow-covered slabs, to the top. Great care should be taken on the slabby sections which are prone to avalanche.

North Castle Gully   230m   I/II*
J.H. Bell and R.G. Napier   4th April 1896
The gully bounding The Castle on the right. Steeper than South Castle Gully, it contains several easy chockstone pitches, often completely covered giving a straightforward snow climb.

Castle Ridge   275m   II (III** at the chimney)
J.N. Collie, W.W. Naismith, G. Thomson and M.W. Traverse   12th April 1895
A fine outing. The easiest of the Nevis Ridges (after Ledge Route) and possible in most conditions. If avalanche conditions prevail it is very difficult (if not impossible) to avoid them on the approaches from beneath, or the traverse from below Carn Dearg Buttress. Start 150m below the point where The Castle Gullies meet and traverse right onto the blunt crest of the ridge by the easiest line. Ascent via ledges, walls and slabs using the easiest line, until the crest is blocked by a band of steep walls. Traverse up and right with difficulty via a flaky chimney in a very exposed position overlooking the North Face to a good ledge and belay. Another difficult pitch leads to an easing in the ridge. Follow more easily to the top of the ridge.
N.B. For teams who are considering descending to the Half Way Lochan (Grid Square 1472) a traverse of the hillside due west (300m) must be made before descending. A number of accidents have occurred in this area with people falling down the North Face, which is immediately on your right at the top of the ridge. In good weather and with enough time, a fine way to round off this ascent it to go up to the north summit of Carn Dearg N.W. (1214m GR 159721) and descend Ledge Route. Alternatively a bearing heading south-west from that summit will lead into the easy Red Burn descent.

CLIMBS ON THE NORTH FACE OF CASTLE RIDGE

This very extensive, steep broken area of rock is the first significant part of the climbing areas as seen across the Allt a'Mhuilinn approach on the right. The left edge is Castle Ridge and to its right is an overhanging section of rock with an obvious groove on its right

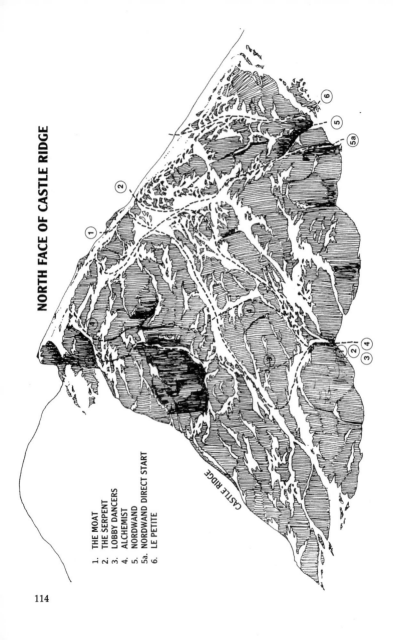

NORTH FACE OF CASTLE RIDGE

CASTLE RIDGE

1. THE MOAT
2. THE SERPENT
3. LOBBY DANCERS
4. ALCHEMIST
5. NORDWAND
5a. NORDWAND DIRECT START
6. LE PETITE

114

(Lobby Dancers). Large snow terraces traverse the face from bottom left towards the shoulder of Carn Dearg N.W.

American Pie   770m   V,5**
D.F. Lang & N.W. Quinn   18th February 1978
Start to the left of The Serpent and climb to the foot of a steep, narrow and hidden right-slanting chimney (30m). Ascend the chimney past a snow bay (30m) and its twisting icy (10m) continuation. Gain the buttress edge and ascend to a snow bay (60m). Climb the short icy groove above to beneath a ramp (15m). Follow the ramp rightwards to the upper amphitheatre (420m). Continue left to a rock band (100m). Go through the rock band on the left (30m). Traverse up right to finish below the top of Castle Ridge (75m).

The Serpent   300m   II
I. Clough, D. Pipes and J. Porter   12th February 1959
The easiest of the routes on the North Face of Castle Ridge. No technical difficulty but serious, with route-finding problems. Above and to the left of the Lunching Stone (Glen Nevis approach) a small right slanting gully gives access to a wide shelf which curves up to the right. After 165m this leads into a couloir which slants rightwards, steeply up the face to come out on the shoulder of Carn Dearg, N.W.

The Moat   500m   II**
I. Sykes, I. Rae and I. Dewar   8th February 1972
A great, highly banked snow ledge runs across the face above The Serpent and gives the line of the climb. Follow The Serpent for 70m then move left to gain the ledge. At the end of the ledge finish by a steep gully. A fine outing across this huge face.

The Lobby Dancers   280m   VI,6***
C. Higgins and A. Kimber   28th February 1977
The left-hand section of the face is dominated by a clean overhanging wall split by a groove. Come in to the foot of the groove from the left by a diagonal ledge or more directly by ice pitches. Climb the groove for 3 pitches to a barrier from where an escape left is made on aid to another groove. Up this groove and on up to Castle Ridge.

Alchemist   270m   VI,5**
A. Paul and D. Sanderson   26th March 1979
Start as for Serpent then follow an icefall to the foot of the groove
system just right of the main groove of Lobby Dancers. Climb the
groove system to the barrier which is crossed by the right wall of a
huge flake, on aid, to a narrow ice chimney. Climb the chimney,
move left then right to a cave. Go right around the arête and follow
the groove to Castle Ridge.

Mist Dancer 50m VI, *(R. Clothier & C. Cartwright 1988)*
This provides a free finish to Alchemist. To the right of the huge
flake, climb a chimney-groove, exit left and go left to join the final
groove of Alchemist.

Last Day in Purgatory   330m   V,5**
C. Higgins and M. Geddes   8th April 1979
Takes an impressive zig-zag line up ledge systems to the clean face
right of The Lobby Dancers.

Nordwand   425m   IV,3*
I. Clough, D. Pipes, B. Sarll, F. Jones and J. Porter   11th February 1959
A fine mixed route. Technical and route-finding problems similar to
those on the Little Brenva Face but no sunshine; a genuine, grim
nordwand atmosphere. Starts fairly well to the right of the centre of
the face at a slight bay. A long vertical snow-filled trench on the
screes below the face often shows the way. Nordwand follows a
short gully up the face for 30m and climbs an ice pitch before
moving left (or works diagonally left below the ice pitch). It continues
to follow the icefalls direct up the centre of the wall crossing the
couloir of The Serpent and continuing by snowfields to the steep
summit rocks. An awkward left rising traverse leads to the top.
Direct Start 100m IV,4** *(G. Suzca and party 1989).* Two pitches just
left of the original start (poorly protected).

Casino Royale   190m   V,5
M. Duff, R. Nowack and A. Bond   29th February 1988
Starts at an obvious thin gully just left of La Petite. Climb the walls,

snow bays and an icefall to below a roof. Move left with difficulty to a thin ice smear in a corner which is followed to the top. Go rightwards at the top to finish.

La Petite   200m   III
D. Pipes and I. Clough   11th February 1959
The climb starts about 30m right of Nordwand and goes up steeply for 40m to gain entry to a couloir. This entry will generally give a 25m ice pitch and then ice glazed rock. The couloir, which leads obliquely right (not obvious from below) should give two more good ice pitches before finishing on the Carn Dearg shoulder.

Le Mechant   140m   IV,4
A. Perkins & M. Duff   9th February 1991
50m right of Le Petite climb a small buttress to belay below a thin gully (35m). Overcome a slab and enter the gully which is followed over an icy bulge (45m). Carry on up icy slabs and grooves to the crest of the buttress and easy ground (80m).

A small buttress well to the right of the face is split by an obvious gully (**Red Gully** *120m II D. Pipes, I.S. Clough, J. Porter, B. Sarll & F. Jones, 1959*).

OUTLYING AREAS
BEN NEVIS

CLIMBS ON STOB BAN (999m) - MAMORES

The North-East face of this steep-sided and rocky peak provides good climbing on ridges, buttresses and gullies when in condition. The shapely summit cone is best seen from Glen Nevis Youth Hostel. An easy approach on a good path is made from the Lower Falls (GR 145684) up the east bank of the Allt Coire a'Mhusgain. Ascend this path to a point opposite the cliffs (GR 155660 - 1½-2 hours), then descend for a short distance to cross the main stream below the cliffs. Approaching the cliffs from this point allows for a good reconnaissance before choosing the correct line of ascent, as the cliffs are more complicated than they may at first appear.

From this point on the path the features are as follows, left to right: East Wing, South Gully, South (summit) Buttress, North Gully, Central Buttress (this appears as a triangular mass of rock set forward and at a lower level than South Buttress) and a long flat col has North Buttress to its right (see diagram).

The routes recommended are as follows:

South Gully	150m	I*
North Gully	150m	I

There are three gully lines on the left (N.E.) flank of Central Buttress. The right-hand two are close together.

No Toddy   150m   III,4
D. Hawthorn, R. Lee and D.N. Williams   April 1986
Climbs the left-hand gully. Start at a small snowfield some distance up the left flank of the buttress. Climb a steep ice pitch to easier ground and a stance on the right. Move back left and ascend the gully easily until it slants right. The right slant has been climbed on an earlier ascent by Malcolm Creasey and party, on that ascent the

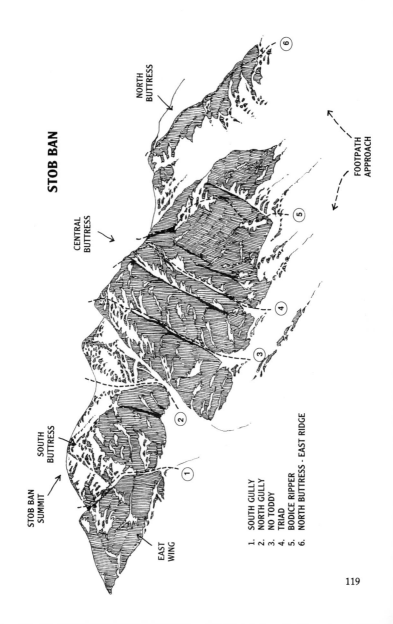

STOB BAN

STOB BAN SUMMIT

SOUTH BUTTRESS

CENTRAL BUTTRESS

NORTH BUTTRESS

EAST WING

FOOTPATH APPROACH

1. SOUTH GULLY
2. NORTH GULLY
3. NO TODDY
4. TRIAD
5. BODICE RIPPER
6. NORTH BUTTRESS - EAST RIDGE

whole climb was graded IV. Traverse left and bridge up a continuation of the lower line. Follow mixed ground to the top of buttress.

The central gully line (no name) was climbed in *1969 by J. Grieve and C. MacNaughton, Grade IV (for 25m), 150m.* Follow the gully and go back left along an easy ramp to gain the crest of the ridge which leads easily to the top of the buttress.

Triad   150m   III
D. Hawthorn, R. Lee and D.N. Williams   April 1986

Climbs the right-hand gully. Start between two narrow rock buttresses. Ascend the gully which gradually steepens and narrows to a chimney. Reach a stance where the right-hand buttress finishes and a ledge runs across the left-hand buttress. Follow a snow ramp on the right, traverse left along a narrow ledge to the buttress crest. Join the easy leftward slanting ramp above as for the previous route. N.B. The buttress between these last two routes has been climbed, (Grade IV).

Bodice Ripper   150m   IV,4*
J. Murphy and D.N. Williams   March 1984

Climbs the large triangular face on the front of Central Buttress. Start right of centre at the foot of an obvious rightward slanting gully. Ascend easily to a prominent leftward slanting ramp. Follow this until it fades and take a poor stance at the foot of a steep and narrow rightward slanting slab. Climb the slab with difficulty to its end and zig-zag up the snow slope above (crux). Continue to the top of the snowfield and ascend the obvious gully. At the top, squeeze up the narrow chimney (Bodice Ripper) leading rightwards. A broad ramp leads left and then by a narrow crest towards the summit.

N.B. A short section of arête at the end of all of the routes on Central Buttress links to the main ridge 200m north of the summit.

North Buttress - East Ridge   200m   II/III
Brown, Hinxman, Tough and Douglas   Easter 1895

This ridge is best approached from the same direction as all the other routes on Stob Ban, with a traverse across the corrie floor, hard right (NW) beneath Central Buttress. Head up towards the route from a flat spot (GR 151660). An excellent exercise in route-finding with tremendous views down Glen Nevis and a fine arête near the top.

Descent
From the summit two fine airy ridges can be used to descend. The North Ridge is the shortest and descends steeply over two subsidiary summits. After approximately 2kms bear north-west to avoid steep grass and rocky outcrops before arriving back at the start point. Alternatively it is possible to descend the steep East Ridge, taking care to avoid the sharply incut gullies to your left (N.W.). After approximately 1km good paths lead back in a northerly direction towards the original ascent path.

N.B. These two descent ridges can also be used as an interesting method of ascent and should really be graded in their final 100m (I).

CLIMBS IN GLEN NEVIS
The following routes are outlined as alternatives for a short day if the weather and conditions (deep freeze for two weeks) allow.

Achintee Gully   200m   II/III
Burns, Newbigging and Raeburn   1904
The obvious deep slit in the hillside above the car park (GR 126730). Requires a fall of snow low down followed by prolonged freezing.

Steall Waterfall   120m   II/III**
I.G. Rowe   1st January 1963
The large waterfall above Steall Hut (GR 177683) can provide good sport, if it freezes enough. Abseil descent using the trees on the left side.

Winter Wall - Polldubh Crags   30m   II/III
As with a number of water weeps on these cliffs a good freeze will bring this climb into condition offering a bit of fun in the valley. Use the Glen Nevis rock climbing guidebook!

AONACH MOR 1221m (GR 193730), and **AONACH BEAG** 1234m (GR 196715)

Along with Ben Nevis and Carn Mor Dearg, their close neighbours, these two peaks form part of the original quartet of 4,000 ft Munro summits that existed in Lochaber before the metric incursion. Until recently they have been reserved for the climber who preferred solitude and long walks. With the development of the Aonach Mor ski slopes by the company of Nevis Range, these peaks will no doubt be subjected to increased interest from climbers with enough brass to catch the Gondola.

Climbing on the flanks of these peaks is varied and interesting. The main areas being the East and West Faces of Aonach Mor and the North - North East and West Faces of Aonach Beag.

Approaches
On foot from the valley!

Aonach Mor West Face
From the north a start should be made at the Nevis Range ski car park, forestry tracks are then followed to emerge at a dam (GR 162759). The Allt Daim is followed until the base of your chosen climb is reached (2 hours).

From the south the approach begins at the head of Glen Nevis (GR 167691). Walk to Steall ruin bridge (GR 186687) and then follow the west bank of the Allt Corrie Guibhsachan to the High Saddle (GR 187722). Traverse the right (east) side of the Allt Daim glen to reach the routes (2^1/$_2$-3 hours). This approach can also be used for routes on the West and North Faces of Aonach Beag. It is also a fine way to approach Carn Mor Dearg if you intend traversing the spectacular arête which links that mountain with Ben Nevis.
N.B. Care should be taken when approaching the Aonach Mor/ Beag col (GR 194720) from either of the previous directions. Many accidents have occurred on this slope, especially in descent.

Aonach Mor East Face
A rough path exists beneath the line of the Gondola on Aonach Mor which may be of use, especially in descent if the last Gondola has

been missed. This is the shortest and quickest approach on foot from the valley.

Aonach Beag

An approach to the eastern facet of Aonach Beag (Stob Coire Bealach GR 206708) and the long N.E. Ridge descending from the main summit of Aonach Beag can be made by continuing past Steall ruin to GR 215690. Then strike up the hill to the north, aiming for the col 731m (1:25,000 map, GR 211705). From here a long and tiring traverse of the corrie must be made to the foot of the N.E. Ridge, 3-$3^1/_2$ hours.

Gondola Approach

Having studied the detail and digested the time involved in the previous methods of approaching these climbs it may become clear that 'shelling out' £5.00 return (1994 prices) is a small price to pay for a day's climbing!

The uplift facilities can be found by turning right (GR 143771) after driving three miles north out of Fort William. It is worth phoning before you leave to find out if the Gondola is running, as it is frequently affected by the strong winds blowing in this area, Tel: Fort William (0397) 705825/6.

The Gondola reaches 650m (GR 186756 approximately). From here it is possible to traverse south-west into the Allt Daim (descend 50m through steep ground) for climbs on the West Face of Aonach Mor, 1-$1^1/_2$ hours.

Three approaches for climbs on the East Face present themselves.

(1) Traverse east beneath Aonach an Nid then south into Coire an Lochain 1-$1^1/_2$ hours.

(2) Ascend the ski slopes to the south aiming for the ridge (Lemming Ridge) above Aonach an Nid on your left (east). The north bounding ridge of Coire An Lochain is then used as a short steep descent, starting where it cuts into Lemming Ridge (GR 193742). Beware of large cornices in this area 1-$1^1/_2$ hours.

(3) Find the top of Easy Gully (Grade I), and either climb or abseil down from its northern rim.

N.B. Due to the large cornices which can form in this area, Approach

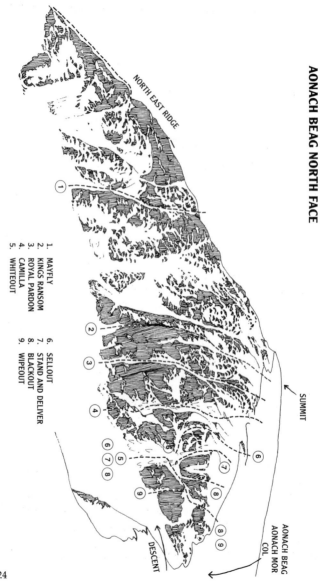

AONACH BEAG NORTH FACE

NORTH EAST RIDGE

1. MAYFLY
2. KINGS RANSOM
3. ROYAL PARDON
4. CAMILLA
5. WHITEOUT

6. SELLOUT
7. STAND AND DELIVER
8. BLACKOUT
9. WIPEOUT

SUMMIT

AONACH BEAG
AONACH MOR
COL

DESCENT

124

Aonach Beag N.E. Ridge and North Face

(1), is recommended if parties are unsure of the cornice formations on Approach (2 & 3). All of the approaches involve traversing steep ground. The corrie is best avoided if avalanche warnings are in force. It may be necessary to abseil back down the cliff if the exit to your chosen route is blocked by a large cornice! Lemming Ridge is a name given by Nevis Range Ski Development. The description of Lemming *(Collins Concise Dictionary, 1988)* is "A member of any group following an unthinking course towards destruction" ... You have been warned!

Aonach Beag Approaches Using the Gondola

Go over the top of Aonach Mor $2^{1/2}$kms ($1^{1/2}$-2 hours) and descend to the Aonach Mor/Beag col previously mentioned (15 minutes). The North Face routes and N.E. Ridge are accessible by descending to the N.E. from this col (beware of large cornices and windslab). Routes on the West Face are reached by descending steeply to the S.W. from the col or approaching on foot from Glen Nevis via the old Steall ruin and the glen of Allt Guibhsachan (2-$2^{1/2}$ hours).

CLIMBS ON AONACH BEAG

Aonach Beag - North Face

The climbs are described from right to left as if descending from the Aonach Mor-Beag col. After 100m a wide icefall is seen on the right. This splits below a steep rock headwall forming a 'Y' shape. Whiteout takes the right branch, Stand and Deliver climbs the prominent central section of the icefall hanging down the wall and Blackout takes the narrow ice chimney 15m to the right. The routes are difficult to protect and a selection of rock pegs and ice gear is recommended for the harder climbs.

Wipeout   60m   IV,6
M. Cooper & C. Bailey   15 April 1994
The icefall right of the first pitch of Whiteout. From rocks on the left of the icefall climb over several steep bulges to rocks directly above.

Whiteout   170m   II
S. Richardson and R. Webb   30th November 1985

From the Aonach Mor/Beag col descend east and take the first prominent icefall on the right and follow it for 50m to a snowfield. Climb this and exit right via a short icefall to another snow slope. This snow slope leads up to a steep buttress with a deep chimney (Blackout) on its left. Climb the right side of the buttress to a final snow slope.

Blackout   120m   IV,5*
J. Dunn and R.G. Webb   21st February 1987
Climb the deep chimney passed by Whiteout in one long hard pitch on its left wall.

Stand And Deliver   120m   V,5*
C. Cartwright and R. Clothier   16th April 1989
The imposing icefall directly above the initial gully of Whiteout. A long and sustained ice pitch.

Sellout   150m   III
R. Webb and S. Richardson   15th April 1989
A left-hand finish to Whiteout. Where Whiteout traverses right, move left below a steep ice-fall (Stand and Deliver), to reach an ice pitch to the left of a rock buttress. Climb this (30m) to reach easier ground above.

About 100m down and left of Whiteout a steep buttress provides some excellent ice climbing.

Camilla   230m   V,5**
R.D. Everett & S.M. Richardson   31st January 1993
A serious ice route which climbs the twin icicles that hang down the overhanging right side of the face at mid-height. Start at the foot of the buttress, 25m right of the prominent icefall taken by Royal Pardon. Climb snow and steep ice to the crest of the buttress (40m). Up the snow slope above and a shallow icy gully to below the twin icicles (50m), belay on the right. Climb the right-hand icicle and easier ground to the crest of the buttress (50m). Continue up ice on the left and a snowfield to the top (90m).

Royal Pardon   220m   VI,6***
R. Webb and S. Richardson   18th February 1987
About 50m right of King's Ransom is a prominent thin ice smear
running down the centre of the buttress. Similar to Smith's Route on
Gardyloo Buttress, but with steeper and thinner ice. Climb a series
of ice falls for 55m to belay at the bottom right-hand side of the
smear. Climb the vertical smear (40m), poor belay on the right. A
short pitch up ice leads to a broad snow couloir (20m). Follow the
couloir for 50m, then left up two good steep ice pitches to the
summit plateau.

King's Ransom   250m   VI,6**
S. Richardson and R. Webb   14th February 1987
Start about 40m left of Royal Pardon. The very left side of the
buttress is split by a narrow gully. Follow the gully for two pitches
until it fades, passing behind a large chockstone and climbing a free
standing ice pillar en route (90m). Belay on a spike below the steep
wall on the left side of the buttress. An escape left is possible from
here, avoiding the difficulties of the upper pillar. Follow a ramp on
the right until it fades, then use aid on the steep wall above to a
second ramp, which is followed delicately to the buttress crest.
Another 120m of climbing follows a fine snow arête and easier
mixed ground to the plateau. A fine and varied route with difficult
mixed climbing in places.

Mayfly   210m   III*
K. Schwartz   9th May 1979
There is a large triangular face between the Aonach Mor/Beag col
and the N.E. Ridge of Aonach Beag. The face has a steep buttress
nearest the col, and easier gully area in the centre and a lower rocky
section. Just left of the centre (GR 197718), an initially wide gully,
marked on its lower right by a rock rib, leads to above the pinnacles
of the N.E. Ridge. This climb takes the gully. After 90m an 18m high
and equally wide icefall is reached and climbed on its right side.
Continue by a much narrower gully above which leads via an

Raeburn's Buttress (III/IV), Ben Nevis. Climber: Alan Kimber

awkward ice bulge to the easier upper section. Finish up N.E. Ridge to the summit.

North-East Ridge   460m   II/III*
J. MacLay, W.W. Naismith and G. Thomson   April 1895
The original climb on Aonach Beag, this long ridge descends well into the corrie below Aonach Beag.

From the col (GR 211705) on the Glen Nevis approach descend for 100m. Head N.N.W. for 1¹/₂-2kms crossing three burns (second and third burns are gorge-like). Arriving at a fourth burn, the ridge is immediately above (1 hour from the col). The toe of the ridge is also approachable from the Aonach Mor/Beag col. The lower section of the ridge is not particularly difficult, but the middle part of the climb is quite narrow, with several pinnacles at half-height, which may be hard in icy conditions. The pinnacles are turned on the right and after regaining the crest an overhung nose is passed on the left. A knife edge snow ridge leads to the broader and easier upper section, finishing about 50m to the north-west of the summit

Stob Coire Bhealaich 1048m (GR 206708)
This peak lies on the south east ridge of Aonach Beag. A sharp ridge leads north, away from the summit to a prominent buttress which falls steeply into the corrie. This buttress provides the following climbs, the best ones being to the left of a prominent narrow slanting snowfield, (The Ramp) which cuts diagonally across the face from left to right and they are best approached from Glen Nevis via the col, G.R. 211705 (2hrs). The routes are described from left to right.

The Clare Effect   120m   IV,3*
S. Kennedy and L. Skoudas   17th March 1989
High on the left side of the face above The Ramp is a prominent right-angled corner. Approach by following The Ramp and enter the corner by steep ice and follow it closely to a large cornice which was tunnelled with difficulty on the first ascent.

The Aonach Eagach Ridge, Glen Coe, (II/III). Climbers descending from the difficult step on Am Bodach at the start of the ridge. This is one of the crux sections of the traverse

Sideslip 180m IV,4
S. Kennedy & D. Ritchie 16th February 1991
Start 10m right of The Clare Effect and climb an obvious corner
rightwards for 60m. An iced slab on the left is followed before
moving back right to reach the fault line which crosses the upper
part of the face. Traverse right along the fault for 10m to reach a large
spike, then up left to a large recessed area. Continue up to open
snow slopes on the right which are followed to the narrow ridge of
The Ramp.

Helter Skelter 240m IV,4 *
S. Kennedy & D. Ritchie 21st February 1993
A serious route which follows a wandering line up the steep face to
the right of Sideslip. Frozen turf and good route finding essential for
success! Start a few metres left of the Ramp and take the first line
leading right onto the face. Climb up and right towards a prominent
rocky beak (belay). Follow a vague groove line above to a shallow
cave. Climb up to a rock band running across the face and follow a
hidden ramp leading back left. Climb back up and right below a
second rock band before pulling out left above by a narrow shelf.
Continue up broken mixed ground to a grassy shelf which leads to
an exposed finish on the narrow ridge of The Ramp.

The Ramp 300m II/III*
*K.V. Crocket, R. Hocky, B.E.H. Maden, R. Miller and R. Pillinger 8th
February 1975*
Just north of the col (GR 211705) a prominent buttress falls towards
the corrie from Stob Coire Bhealaich (GR 206708 - 1:25,000 map).
Left of the crest of the buttress is a long tapering snow slope.
Although it appears to be a couloir, it is in fact a ramp passing
through a steep face. At the top a further 60m of ridge (exposed on
the left) leads to the summit.

Blinkers Buttress 300m II
R. Everett, N. Barratt and S. Richardson 26th February 1989
The difficulties are avoidable but the climb provides a fine excursion
in remote and beautiful surroundings. Start in a snow gully 50m to

the right of The Ramp start. (A Direct Start grade IV is possible a little to the left.) Snow leads to a belay beneath the steep crest of the buttress (50m). Climb a series of icy grooves to the right of the crest above (50m). Follow the ridge to the top and the upper part of The Ramp.

CLIMBS ON AONACH MOR

East Face. Coire nan Lochain

These routes come into condition quickly and early in the season due to their altitude. It should be possible to climb a number of routes in a day, as they are short and access is fairly easy. Later in the winter or after heavy snowfalls the routes will bank out and huge cornices form over some of the climbs and access routes. Some of the climbs may have been climbed by R.A.F. parties in the sixties and never recorded. The climbs are described from left to right as the climber faces the corrie.

Hidden Gully   120m   II*
R. Webb and C. Rice   21st January 1989
At the south end of the corrie, some way left of the open descent gully (Easy Gully) is an attractive narrow twisting couloir.

The following three climbs are located on **The Prow**, a buttress which lies approximately 100m left of Easy Gully and just left of a distinctive deep gully.

The Betrayal   90m   IV,4
S. Kennedy and D. Ritchie   28th March 1990
The left-hand of the two parallel grooves on the front of the buttress. Follow the groove over bulges to a small snow bay immediately beneath the prow. Move steeply and awkwardly left to reach easier ground and cornice finish.

The Guardian   90m   IV,5*
S. Kennedy and D. Ritchie   28th March 1990
Climb the right-hand of the two parallel grooves and a prominent flake chimney to steep but easier ground.

AONACH MOR EAST FACE

COIRE NAN LOCHAIN (RIGHT SIDE)

1. EASY GULLY
2. MUDDY WATERS
3. TEMPERANCE UNION BLUES
4. WHITE SHARK
5. TINSEL TOWN
6. TUNNEL VISION
7. MORWIND
8. TURF WALK

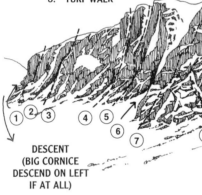

DESCENT
(BIG CORNICE
DESCEND ON LEFT
IF AT ALL)

9. ROARING FORTIES
10. TYPHOON
11. HURRICANE ARÊTE
12. LEFT TWIN
13. FORGOTTEN TWIN

Stirling Bridge   70m   VI,7**
S. Kennedy and D. Ritchie   4th April 1990
An excellent route with a memorable first pitch (steep and strenuous).
Follow the prominent right-angled corner near the right edge of the
buttress, going right near the top. A short groove above and a block
belay on the left leads to easier ground below the cornice.

A chimney 30m left of Easy Gully is climbed by **The Web** 100m II/
III *C. Grindley and S. Kennedy 25th November 1989*. A further 20m left
again is an icefall taken by **Nausea** 90m II/III *J. Naismith and C.
Watkins 25th November 1989*. Both routes bank out after heavy snow.

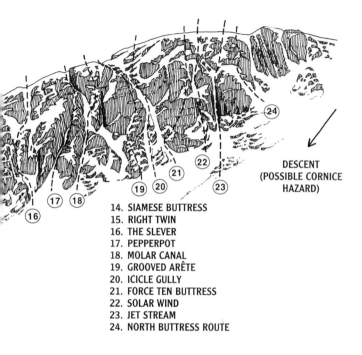

14. SIAMESE BUTTRESS
15. RIGHT TWIN
16. THE SLEVER
17. PEPPERPOT
18. MOLAR CANAL
19. GROOVED ARÊTE
20. ICICLE GULLY
21. FORCE TEN BUTTRESS
22. SOLAR WIND
23. JET STREAM
24. NORTH BUTTRESS ROUTE

DESCENT
(POSSIBLE CORNICE
HAZARD)

Easy Gully   100m   I
The broad snow gully which cuts deep into the plateau and can
provide a useful descent route. A large cornice can often be avoided
on the right in ascent. Beware of off piste skiers!

The area between Easy Gully and Tunnel Vision is known as
Ribbed Walls. Many of the routes bank out and a large impassable
cornice often forms, in which case an exit can usually be made just
to the left of the final tower of Gondola With the Wind.

Muddy Waters   90m   III
C. Jones, S. Kennedy and D. Ritchie   17th November 1990

About 10m right of Easy Gully is an obvious chimney high on the buttress which is climbed trending right towards the cornice. The lower section is often banked out.

Barrel Buttress   60m   IV,4
S. Kennedy and S. Thirgood   7th February 1993.
Between Muddy Waters and Temperance Union Blues is a small recess with a sharp narrow arête on its right and a broad buttress on the left. Climb the buttress directly starting just to its right and avoiding the steep wall at the top on the left.

Nid Arête   90m   IV,5*
S. Kennedy and S. Thirgood   7th February 1993
A well protected mixed route which climbs the groove line on the left side of the narrow arête to the right of Barrel Buttress. The groove is climbed direct, taking the furthest corner on the right overlooking the final section of Temperance Union Blues.

Temperance Union Blues 90m   III
S. Richards, G. Armstrong, C. Millar and J. Owens   18th February 1989
50m to the right of Easy Gully the cliff is split by a deep cleft at half-height. Climb either of two converging lines to the bottom of the cleft (45m). Ascend the cleft, exiting where it steepens on to a ramp which is followed to the cornice (45m).

Pernille   70m   III
C. Jones and A. Taylor   27th March 1990.
The buttress immediately right of the deep cleft of Temperance Union Blues. Gain an obvious scoop just right of the cleft. Continue up right to a steep left-trending ramp which is followed to a snowy bay and exit rightwards to reach the cornice.

Immediately left of the wide gully of Tunnel Vision, two buttresses are separated by a snowy amphitheatre. On the better defined right-hand buttress is the fine line of Gondola With the Wind. The main feature of the left-hand buttress is two icefalls which form down the left side.

Aquafresh   100m   IV,4*
N. Marshall and D. Ritchie   26th March 1990.
40m left of Tunnel Vision. Climb the left-hand icefall, trending left up mixed ground to finish.

White Shark   110m   IV,4***
C. Millar and R. Webb   27th January 1990.
The right-hand icefall - a splendid climb. Climb the shallow gully and a steep slabby corner at mid height to a ledge. Follow the steep ice pitch which forms down the corner to easier ground.

Tinsel Town   110m   V,4**
S. Kennedy and P. Mills   3rd February 1991.
Follows the groove-line left of Gondola With the Wind. Start 10m right of White Shark. Follow a groove system just right of the buttress crest, then a chimney to a stance on the left (40m). Go back right to the main groove and climb steep mixed ground to below the cornice (50m). A long traverse right may be necessary to outflank the huge cornice!!

Remora   100m   III,4
R. Reid and R. Webb   24th February 1990.
Follow the first pitch of Tinsel Town, then up left below the steep crest of the upper buttress and belay above the icefall of White Shark. Easy snow to finish.

Gondola With the Wind   125m   IV,5**
S. Kennedy and S. Thirgood   30th December 1989
A good mixed climb up the right side of the buttress, just left of Tunnel Vision, with an exciting finish. Starts up a short groove 8m left of Tunnel Vision, gaining a small amphitheatre and exit on the right (45m). A system of shallow grooves close to the buttress edge is followed, then spiral right round the side of the tower to reach a steep corner (35m), which is followed with difficulty to easier ground (45m).

Tunnel Vision   120m   III
S. Richardson and R. Everett   22nd January 1989
The wide gully between the Ribbed Walls and Central Buttress. Start at the foot of the gully immediately left of Morwind. An initial narrows leads to a snow bay with three possible exits. Climb ice smears up the wall at the back of the bay with interest, in an exposed position, to a steep cornice exit. In full conditions the wall may bank up to a frightening angle and the cornice becomes impassable. The left branch would provide a steep and technical alternative (Grade III/IV) and it should always be possible to climb the right branch to reach the easy upper section of Morwind.

Moving right, the area between Tunnel Vision and Left Twin is known as **Central Buttress.** Some of the finest mixed climbing on the mountain is situated here. The cornice can be massive, but a vague snow arête on the final slopes often provides a possible exit. Failing that it is possible to traverse right for 50m and descend the gully of Forgotten Twin.

Shelf Route   110m   III
S. Kennedy and S. Thirgood   9th March 1990
Start in a small bay up left of the lowest point of the buttress. Move up and right to a steep groove which is followed to a narrow shelf on the left of the buttress crest and overlooking Tunnel Vision. Follow the shelf until it is possible to break out right onto the buttress crest and follow Morwind to finish.

Morwind   150m   III,4***
R. Everett and S. Richardson   10th January 1988
A fine mixed climb taking a direct line up a series of grooves on the crest of Central Buttress, starting from the lowest rocks about 30m left of Typhoon. A good technically interesting climb. Climb a short gully leading to a shallow chimney line with several tricky steps on the crest. This leads to a small bay beneath a cave after two pitches. Exit right up mixed ground to easier slopes beneath the cornice (which could be very large late in the season).

Turf Walk   150m   III,4*
R.D. Everett and C. Grant   25th November 1989
Good mixed climbing on the right-slanting fault line which crosses
the front side of the buttress on the left. Start 15m right of Morwind,
following a left slanting gully to belay in a bay below the fault.
Follow the fault to ledges leading right. Step right, then up and left,
to belay below steep grooves on the left of the central depression.
Follow the groove on the left, stepping left onto the exposed prow
and continuing to easier ground above.

Roaring Forties   150m   IV,4*
R.D. Everett , S.M. Richardson and J.C. Wilkinson   2nd March 1991
A fine varied route which climbs the icefall which forms in the
depression in the centre of the face. Not in condition as often as other
routes in this area. Start 5m left of the corner of Typhoon. Follow icy
grooves to a recess (45m) and climb the steep back wall by a groove
on the right (25m). The icefall is followed (50m) to easier ground
20m below the cornice.

Typhoon   130m   IV,4***
R. Everett and S. Richardson   14th January 1989
This excellent climb takes a direct line up the grooves just left of
Hurricane Arête. Start 15m left of the deep gully of Left Twin. Climb
the lower slabby grooves to a belay at the base of a chimney (40m).
Climb the chimney and the groove past an overhang (30m). Continue
direct on steep ice to exit on to the final slopes (40m). A further 20m
leads to the top.

Hurricane Arête   140m   VI,7**
S. Richardson and R. Everett   4th March 1989
The slabby Central Buttress, left of Left Twin, is the highest section
of crag in the corrie. On its right-hand side is a steep arête, with
several overhangs in its upper section, which forms the left wall of
Left Twin. This hard climb takes an intricate line through the
overhangs just left of the arête. Start mid-way between Typhoon
and Left Twin.
    Climb iced slabs (30m) to a short left-slanting gully. Climb this,

then up right along a narrow ramp to a small ledge (20m). Belay below a prominent overhang, just left of a right-facing corner which is capped by another overhang. Pull over the roof directly above the belay onto a steep slab, and follow a left-slanting crack to reach a prominent spike. Go right below an overhanging wall to a small snow bay (20m). A short but difficult pitch.

Climb grooves on the left to the final overhangs which are climbed by bridging up left towards easier ground (50m). Another 20m leads to the cornice.

Right of **Central Buttress** are two steep narrow buttresses **(Split and Siamese)**, bordered by three deep gullies. The left side of Split Buttress is characterised by the deep chimney of The Split containing several jammed blocks which are a good reference point in misty weather.

Left Twin   120m   III***
R. Everett and S. Richardson   22nd January 1989
The obvious gully a few metres left of Forgotten Twin and immediately right of Central Buttress. It is climbed direct and is comparable in quality and difficulty to SC Gully in Glen Coe. The right side of the gully is steeper and harder than the left.

The Split   130m   III,4**
S. Richardson and R. Everett   19th January 1989
The left-hand side of the buttress left of Forgotten Twin is split by a deep chimney. Start at the foot of the buttress and climb the introductory chimney to snow slopes to the right of Left Twin (25m). Enter the deep chimney and continue under several large jammed blocks until it is possible to exit to the left some 4m below the final overhang. Continue up the arête to belay (45m). Climb easy snow leftwards to join Left Twin (50m).

Lickety Split   130m   IV,5**
G. Mulhemann and S.M. Richardson   2nd December 1989
A fine, varied mixed route. Climb the icefall directly below the gully of Forgotten Twin, to a stance below the right-facing corner on the

right side of the lower half of Split Buttress (30m). Follow the corner to a stance (20m) and continue up the steep wall above, passing two overhangs to a rock ridge overlooking Left Twin (20m). Up the ridge to easier ground and the cornice (60m).

Slick Mick's Groove　　　130m　　IV,5*
N. Hitchings, M. Hardwick and A.V. Saunders　27th February 1992
A good technical climb. Climb the first pitch of Lickety Split, then move left around the rib to gain the small left-facing groove left of the crux corner of Lickety Split. Climb the corner (hard) and exit with difficulty onto a ledge. Continue to the final ridge of Lickety Split (40m) and the ridge to the top (60m).

Forgotten Twin　　.　　120m　　I/II
R. Everett and S. Richardson　22nd January 1989
The gully between the buttresses of Split and Siamese. A short leftward ramp from the foot of Right Twin leads to an easy gully with a couple of steeper stretches before the cornice exit. If the cornices are impassable it should be possible to reach and descend this climb from all the routes in the central area.

Siamese Buttress　　　120m　　II**
S. Richardson and R. Everett　19th February 1989
The well defined buttress left of Right Twin provides an enjoyable scramble. Harder (Grade III) if started up the steep corners on the left.

Right Twin　　　120m　　II***
S. Richardson and R. Everett　22nd January 1989
The gully on the right of Siamese Buttress. About $1^{1/2}$m wide with vertical side walls, it gives an enjoyable traditional climb with steep sections at the bottom and at mid-height. Exit left at the top.

The following four routes start in a large bay about 50m left of Grooved Arête.

The Slever   100m   III,4
S. Kennedy and D. Ritchie   2nd March 1991
The large icefall on the left margin of the bay is climbed in one long
pitch to easier ground. Then move right into a small gully and easily
towards the cornice.

Pepperpot   100m   III,4
R. Lee and N. Wright   January 1990
Right of The Slever in the top left-hand corner of the bay is a steep
icy chimney. Follow this and finish up a gully on the left.

Golden Promise   100m   VI,7
B. Davison, S. Kennedy and S. Venables   23rd February 1992
A difficult mixed route which climbs the steep groove line at the top
right-hand side of the bay. Climb the easier lower snow gully to a
large block belay on the right at the foot of the main difficulties
(45m). Climb the steep groove above, pulling over a large bulge at
20m, to reach a small cul-de-sac. Exit by a groove on the left and
easier grooves above to belay just short of the upper gully of Molar
Canal (45m). Climb the gully to the top (10m).

Molar Canal   100m   III
C. Jones and S. Kennedy   25th January 1990
Approximately 35m left of Grooved Arête is a gully, deep and wide
in the top section. Climb a short icefall and grooves into the gully
which is climbed towards the cornice which might be impassable
direct. In which case a long traverse left is required.

North Buttress is the final section at the northern side of the corrie.
It is separated from Molar Canal by two narrow ribs and is made up
of three distinct buttresses, cut by the deep Icicle Gully to the left and
the clean groove of Jet Stream on the right.

Grooved Arête   130m   IV,5***
S. Richardson and R. Everett   26th November 1988
This superb climb takes the narrow arête immediately left of Icicle
Gully. Start at the foot of the gully, gain the arête to the left and
follow this, easily at first, then with increasing interest up grooves

on its left side before moving back right to belay below a steep tower (45m). Climb a series of steep grooves on the crest of the tower until it is possible to move left to a ledge. Climb the short vertical corner above with difficulty, exiting on the right (35m). Regain the crest and continue more easily to the plateau (50m). Excellent technical climbing.

Icicle Gully   130m   III
R. Everett and S. Richardson   26th November 1988
The gully between Grooved Arête and Force Ten Buttress. Climb the gully line with interest to a belay on the right (50m). Take the wider line to the right of a narrow groove (which is bounded by Grooved Arête to the left). Climb this until it narrows and steepens at an icicle, which leads to a snow bay (50m). Continue up the mixed ground above (30m).

Force Ten Buttress   140m   III,4
R.Everett and S.Richardson   3rd December 1988
This good mixed climb takes the buttress between Icicle Gully and Jet Stream. Climb mixed ground just left of the crest then move right to a belay at the foot of a short chimney where the buttress steepens (45m). Climb the chimney then step right to climb a short difficult crack (30m). Now climb mixed ground, mainly just to the right of the crest, to join a gully which rises to a col where the buttress merges into the final slopes (40m). The climb is technically hard for the grade, with several short, difficult, well protected sections, but the rock is very friendly!

Direct Finish   70m   V,6
B. Ottewell and S. Wilshaw   16th February 1993
Instead of going right of the crest after the second pitch follow snowy slabs up left to a small outcrop overlooking Icicle Gully (50m). Now move up right over slabs to a large block on the arête (22m). Move back left up a turfy corner and the overhanging corner on the right which is climbed by a crack on the right. Continue by sustained climbing to easier ground (35m).

In a bay between Force Ten Buttress and North Buttress are two prominent gully lines which form ice easily and being in the shade, stay in condition throughout the winter.

Solar Wind   110m   IV,4*
R.D. Everett and S.M. Richardson   8th March 1992
Start close beneath Force Ten Buttress and follow the obvious left-hand chimney to a snow patch (45m). Ascend the steep square-cut groove above, exiting left near the top to reach and climb the continuation gully, and belay where Force Ten Buttress merges with the final slopes (40m). 25m remain to the cornice.

Jet Stream   100m   IV,4***
R. Everett and S. Richardson   3rd December 1988
This is the narrow gully immediately left of North Buttress (which forms an icicle icefall in its lower part) about 50m left of the northerly bounding corrie ridge. Climb the gully over several steep sections to a snow bay (45m). Exit right up a steep awkward wall to easier ground which leads to below the cornice (45m). Up to the cornice and over the top (10m). Excellent climbing. When fully formed, the icefall which forms in the headwall would make an exciting and fitting direct finish.

To the right of Solar Wind is a chimney which can be used as an alternative start to either of the previous climbs **Guides Variation** *(45m IV,4 S. Allan & D. Etherington February 1992)*.

North Buttress Route   85m   III
C. Jones, S. Kennedy and R. Williamson   25th January 1990.
A quick route at the end of the day. Avoid the steep lower section of the buttress which is characterised by a prominent icefall. Start in a bay 20m up right from the foot of the buttress. Climb grooves up left to the crest which is followed to the top.

CLIMBS ON THE WEST FACE OF AONACH MOR

The West Face of Aonach Mor presents several granite ridges of moderate angle 400m high. The steepest of these are directly below the summit cairn, and being in a slightly recessed bay, they are hidden from many viewpoints. The climbs provide excellent mountaineering routes in a wild and remote setting.

Golden Oldy 400m II
A. Kimber 21st December 1979
Follow the leftmost buttress which becomes better defined higher up.

Western Rib 400m II/III**
S. Richardson 17th December 1988
From below, the second buttress from the left appears as a flying buttress joining the third, broader buttress (Daim Buttress). A delightful long route with sustained interest, never very hard.

Spare Rib Gully 300m III
C. Bailey, M. Cooper & R. Hudson 25th January 1993
Climb the lowest gully between Western Rib and Daim Buttress in three pitches to easier ground (100m). Move right from the gully onto a rocky buttress which is followed to the summit.

Daim Buttress 400m II/III
R. Everett, N. Barratt and S. Richardson 25th February 1989
This is the third buttress from the left, characterised by a prominent slab just above half-height. Start directly below the slab at the foot of the buttress. The first 200m gives enjoyable mixed climbing up snow and rocky corners to ledges at the foot of the slab. Move left and climb cracks on the left edge of the slab to a platform (50m). Take the cracks and corners up the buttress above (50m). Scrambling leads to the top.

Solitaire 400m II
R.D. Everett and S.M. Richardson 1st January 1990.
The right-hand ridge, starting just left of a deep gully. It is slightly easier than the other routes hereabouts. A good scramble in the summer (Difficult)!!
   Many more variations are possible in this area.

AONACH BEAG WEST FACE

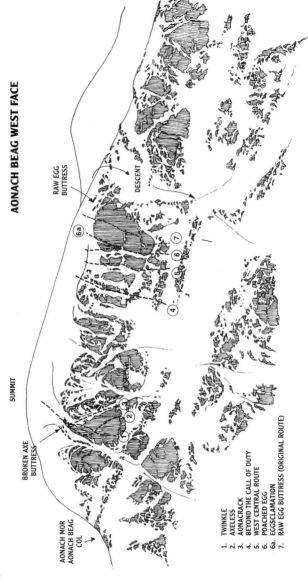

SUMMIT

BROKEN AXE
BUTTRESS

AONACH MOR
AONACH BEAG
COL

RAW EGG
BUTTRESS

DESCENT

1. TWINKLE
2. AXELESS
3. AONACRACK
4. BEYOND THE CALL OF DUTY
5. WEST CENTRAL ROUTE
6. POACHED EGG
6a. EGGSCLAMATION
7. RAW EGG BUTTRESS (ORIGINAL ROUTE)

CLIMBS ON AONACH BEAG WEST FACE

In clear weather the main features of this face are easily seen from the top of N.E. Buttress or the Abseil Posts on Ben Nevis and climbers in that area could help themselves by spying out the lines when on Ben Nevis. Moving south from the Aonach Beag/Mor col the first feature is a broad gully bounded on its right by Broken Axe Buttress which has another deep easy gully on its right. Right of this gully is a lot of broken ground which forms several icefalls before arriving at the most prominent buttress, Raw Egg Buttress (approx. GR 191711) some 700m south-west of the col. The climbs are described as if approaching from the col. An approach from Glen Nevis via Steall ruin and the Allt Guibhsachan is also possible (2-2½ hrs).

Twinkle   150m   IV,5**
R. Everett and S. Richardson   20th February 1988
An excellent mixed route which follows the crest of Broken Axe Buttress directly. Technically quite hard for the grade, but well protected and with several escapes possible to easier ground. Climb a chimney-groove to the left of the steep wall left of Axeless, then move right to belay above the wall (30m). Climb the open groove above to a small ledge, step right and climb the continuation groove to a small col junction with Axeless (40m). Step right to a steep corner. Climb this and the overhanging chimney above then continue direct to join the final easy arête (50m). Follow Axeless to the top.

Axeless   150m   III*
R. Webb and R. Everett   16th January 1988
This climb takes an indirect but interesting line up Broken Axe Buttress. Start at a steep wall at the foot of the buttress in a small snow bay. Climb a groove on the right to a ledge overlooking the gully. Step right on to steep ice and climb up to snow which leads back left to the crest of the buttress at a col. Move left to avoid the steep step above, then trend back right to gain a fine ridge which leads to the top.

Aonacrack   150m   IV,5*
J. Ashbridge and S.M. Richardson   21st March 1993
A good mixed climb which climbs the prominent crack on the right side of the buttress. Start close to the small snowy bay right of Axeless. Follow a ramp awkwardly to the base of the crack (15m). Climb the crack and a steep bulge to a ledge below a huge perched block . Follow a crack on the left side of the block to a belay on the top (25m). Continue in the crack and a steep bulging groove to a ledge (40m). Follow the broken ridge easily to the snow arête of Twinkle (40m), which is followed for another 30m.

Beyond the Call of Duty   150m   III,4
R. Everett and S. Richardson   20th February 1988
This climb takes the prominent series of icefalls which form in the centre of the face between Raw Egg and Broken Axe Buttresses. The first is easy angled, the second is a standing pillar approached from the right and the third starts steeply but eases higher up. Snow slopes then lead to the top.

West Central Route   150m   II
R. Everett and R. Webb   16th January 1988
A fine open mountaineering line to the right of Beyond the Call. Follow open grooves to belay at the right end of the rock wall which is to the right of the second pitch of Beyond the Call. Climb the icefall to the right, then follow snow to a right-facing groove high on the face. Follow this then snow to the top.

Poached Egg   150m   II**
R.G. Webb and J. Dunn   21st February 1987
The groove system left of Raw Egg Buttress.

Eggsclamation   150m   II
S. Richardson and R. Everett   5th April 1987
Immediately left of Raw Egg Buttress is an icy couloir. Follow this over short steps until the main line trends left (Poached Egg). Climb a short wall to gain the steeper direct continuation which finishes next to the final rocks of the buttress.

Aonach Wall   150m   V,6*
R. Everett and S. Richardson   27th March 1988
This climb takes a direct line just to the right of the left arête of Raw Egg Buttress, taking in enjoyable technical climbing of steadily increasing difficulty. Start to the left of Raw Egg Buttress below the steep tower with the prominent perched block. Climb up and avoid the tower on the right to belay by the notch - as for Raw Egg Buttress (55m). Climb directly up via a short corner to gain snow below a longer corner which leads to the crest of the arête (40m). Easy snow leads to the base of the headwall (20m). Climb a groove and wide crack straight above to a ledge (20m). Move right to gain the obvious V-groove which provides the only line up the final wall. Climb this with difficulty to the top (15m).

Raw Egg Buttress   180m   IV,4**
R. Everett and S. Richardson   5th April 1987
A good, well-protected mixed climb with several short difficult steps which takes a line up the front face trending from left to right. Start to the left of the lowest rocks on the left side of the crag. Climb an icy groove to below an overhanging corner, and then traverse right below a steep wall until it is possible to climb it (30m). Now trend up and left over mixed ground to belay next to a notch in the ridge on the left, formed by a tower with a prominent perched block (50m). Follow the icy groove line above for two long pitches, always trending right, over several steep steps and corners (85m). The last pitch takes a steep corner to the left of a steep wall and has a difficult exit (15m).

Salmonella   125m   VII,8**
R. Everett and S. Richardson   23rd March 1991
A very hard mixed climb. Start about 30m up and right of the previous climb, below a prominent right-facing corner which cuts the lower tier and is gained by moderate mixed ground. Climb the overhanging corner for 20m, then continue more easily to a ledge and easy ground (35m). Possible escape down to the right. Scramble up to the obvious V-groove (15m). Climb the groove past a ledge, then continue up a chimney to belay below the prominent

overhanging off-width (40m). Climb the off-width to a ledge (10m), then gain an alcove and pull over an overhang to easier ground (25m).

Well up and right of the previous route is an impressive rock wall which has a couple of good summer climbs on it. The right edge of this wall is defined by a deep gully which steepens into a narrow chimney, capped by three giant chockstones (Ruadh Eigg Chimney).

Ruadh Eigg Chimney   60m   IV,5*
R. Everett, G. Muhlemann and S. Richardson   28th March 1992
Follow snowy steps to the foot of the chimney, then up over the chockstones and ice on the left wall.

Never A Dull Moment   70m   IV,6
R. Everett and S. Richardson   1st January 1990
Right of Ruadh Eigg chimney is another gully, steep at mid height. Follow the gully past an amphitheatre, then the rock groove on the right, then back left to easier ground.

GLEN COE

GLEN COE (See map on back endpaper)

The peaks of Glen Coe are all considerably lower than those of Ben Nevis and the Aonachs and good conditions are therefore less certain. Nonetheless, this area provides a wider range of route choice, especially in the lower grades, than does The Ben. The ridges which abruptly separate the deep glens and corries are all fine outings, whilst the ridge and corrie walls provide excellent winter climbing to all standards. Indeed it could be argued that the 'Coe' is at the leading edge of modern winter climbing on Scotland's west coast, especially where mixed routes are concerned.

Recent developments of the techniques of torquing (jamming and twisting both axe and hammer into steep, rocky, snow-covered natural crack lines, in order to make progress) have pushed standards of difficulty upwards in Glen Coe. Albeit away from the traditional snow/ice climb. Generally the ice climbing in Glen Coe when in condition will be of the frozen waterfall/drainage weeps variety, unlike Ben Nevis which provides more frozen atmospheric rime ice cover due to its higher elevation.

Another major advantage over Ben Nevis are the shorter approaches, especially when starting from higher up the glen. Some routes on 'The Buachaille' for example can be started after only an hour's walk. Descent routes from all of the peaks should be treated with extreme care due to the steep and rocky nature of this area.

CLIMBS ON THE WEST FACE OF AONACH DUBH

The west face of Aonach Dubh which faces Clachaig Inn is a vast and complex series of buttresses and gullies. If the snow level is low the face comes quickly into condition and so provides one of the more popular cliffs in the Glen. The buttresses are split horizontally into three tiers by Middle Ledge, between the lowest and middle tiers, and The Rake, between middle and upper tiers. Splitting the face vertically are six main gullies numbered from left to right and there are two scoops which split the main mass of the middle tier. The best approach is from the

149

STOB COIRE NAN LOCHAN

AONACH DUBH WEST FACE

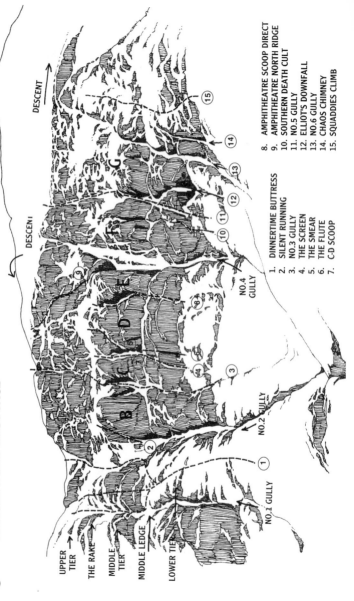

UPPER TIER
THE RAKE
MIDDLE TIER
MIDDLE LEDGE
LOWER TIER

DESCENT

DESCENT

DESCENT

NO.1 GULLY

NO.2 GULLY

NO.4 GULLY

1. DINNERTIME BUTTRESS
2. SILENT RUNNING
3. NO.3 GULLY
4. THE SCREEN
5. THE SMEAR
6. THE FLUTE
7. C-D SCOOP

8. AMPHITHEATRE SCOOP DIRECT
9. AMPHITHEATRE NORTH RIDGE
10. SOUTHERN DEATH CULT
11. NO.5 GULLY
12. ELLIOT'S DOWNFALL
13. NO.6 GULLY
14. CHAOS CHIMNEY
15. SQUADDIES CLIMB

bridge (GR 137566) on the main road at Clachaig road end and up to the right of the stream until above the waterfalls. Cross the stream and gain access to the climbs. The safest descent is to go over the ridge and down into Coire nan Lochan or right into Coire nam Beith but the quickest way, in good visibility, is by the easy upper part of No.2 Gully and the lower part of Dinner-time Buttress.

Dinner-time Buttress   335m   I/II**

Lies on the left-hand side of the face below the col between the Nose of Aonach Dubh and Stob Coire nan Lochan. It is defined by the vague No.1 Gully on the left and by the deep watercourse of No.2 Gully on the right. Except for the final section it is mainly grass with short sections of scrambling. Can be used to approach the climbs on Stob Coire nan Lochan. A good bad weather route.

Various options can be found on reaching the final rocky section, and all are worthwhile.

(1)   Traverse left into No.1 Gully. Grade I/II.
(2)   Climb a short awkward chimney in the frontal face of the buttress between No.1 and 2 gullies, followed by some interesting scrambling. Grade II.
(3)   Traverse right into No.2 Gully. Grade 1.
(4)   Climb an icy gully up left at the point where No.2 Gully is entered. Grade II.

Silent Running   120m   IV/V
M. Duff and R. Nowack   7th February 1986
An ice smear forms on the north wall of B Buttress where Dinner-time Buttress joins No 2 Gully. Gain the smear by a ramp.

Middle Ledge   II
Gained from No.2 Gully, the ledge gives an exposed if easy traverse. The only difficulty lies in the initial pitch out of No.2 Gully. On reaching No.4 Gully ascend the middle section of the gully without difficulty and escape left along the Rake. Impressive scenery.

Cyclops   105m   III/IV
H. MacInnes and party   January 1970
At the start of Middle Ledge a steep corner goes directly up B Buttress. Climb this to easier ground. Take the chimney line above to again an eye in the buttress. From the other side of the eye climb iced rocks to the top.

The Pinnacle Face   90m   III/IV*
K.V. Crocket and C. Stead   31st January 1971
Start 10m right of a chimney which itself is just right of the groove of Cyclops. Just left of the buttress edge follow a slab awkwardly up left to the crest. Climb the crest for two pitches to a steep wall which is climbed on the right to the easier ground of The Rake above.

No.3 Gully   300m   II/III*
Crofton and Evans   March 1934
This gully immediately right of B Buttress is shallow and rather indefinite except where it cuts through the middle tier. Often gives a good ice pitch at the start. The top part, often avoided by The Rake, is well worth doing.

The Screen   75m   V,5**
D. Bathgate and J. Brumfitt   February 1965
The obvious large icefall which forms over the lowest tier of rocks to the right of No.3 Gully. Climb for 25m to an icicle recess (good runner), step left and move up to rock belays on the left. Trend right to Middle Ledge. An enjoyable and popular route.

The Smear   75m   III/IV*
I. Clough and party   26th March 1969
This icefall lies on the right wall of No.3 Gully where it cuts the middle tier. A pleasant climb which can provide a suitable continuation to The Screen.

The Flute   75m   V,5**
D. Cuthbertson and E. Todd   1979
Just to the right of The Screen is a narrow icy chimney which gives the line of the climb.

C Buttress   150m   II
J. McArtney, A. Smith, A. Thompson, A. Taylor and K. Withall   February 1969
Enter by the lower part of B Buttress and Middle Ledge and climb the middle tier by a short, wide chimney. Continue up the well defined crest.

C-D Scoop   150m   II**
D. Bathgate and J. Brumfit   February 1965

The easy gully splitting the middle tier above The Screen.

D Buttress   150m   II/III
I. Clough, J. Choat, J. Friend, P. Mallinson and D. Power   February 1969
Climb a steep icy gangway just to the right of C-D Scoop from the Middle Ledge. Above, zig-zag ramps and ledges lead to the crest where a steep grooved wall leads to easier ground.

Amphitheatre Scoop Direct 240m   V,5***
I.S. Clough, G. Lowe and J. Hardie   February 1966
To the right of the middle tier of D Buttress is a well defined gully with a steep ice pitch above Middle Ledge. Start beneath the lower tier directly below this gully. Climb the lower tier by a steep ice chimney (crux) and continue by the ice pitch to gain the easy upper gully. One of the best climbs on the face.

Amphitheatre North Ridge 100m   II
I. Clough and party   27th January 1969
Starts above and slightly right of the easy upper gully of Amphitheatre Scoop and goes up a series of cracks and grooves in the fine crest.

No.4 Gully   300m   III/IV*
J. Brown and D. Whillans   December 1952
The obvious deep gully near the centre of the face has several pitches in the lower part but unfortunately rarely has its deep-cleft finish in true condition. Gives an interesting route when combined with Christmas Couloir.

Christmas Couloir   240m   III/IV*
I. Clough and D.G. Roberts   25th December 1965
From the easy middle section of No.4 Gully move up and right to the foot of the icefall which drops from an obvious couloir to the right of No.4 Gully onto The Rake. Climb the icefall by a long pitch and continue more easily to a choice of three steep finishes.

Christmas Eaves   90m   III/IV
A variation to Christmas Couloir which takes a central line into a corner when opposite the base of the ramp leading on to The Rake. Climb up right-wards to regain the main route on the snow slopes above.

Southern Death Cult   150m   VI**
J. Tinker and K. Howett   3rd February 1984
Start at a recess 15m left of No.5 Gully and follow the overhanging fault diagonally right via vegetation to a hanging stance under the roofs at their right end (30m). Climb icicles through the roof and exit right to a shallow cave below a rock barrier (40m). Go up left to an ice weep which cuts through the bulge and groove and continue up easy slopes past trees to the upper rock band. Belay below the iced chimney (The Vent, Severe) (35m). Ascend a vertical icicle in the chimney and overhanging groove, then continue up snow to a large cave (45m). Easy gully to the top.

No.5 Gully   300m   III*
A. Fyffe, C. MacInnes and N. Clough   18th February 1969
A gigantic icicle forms on the overhanging wall directly below this gully, so start to the left at the short leftward slanting gully. Climb this gully (crux) to a cave. Exit by a steep ice wall on the right and head up right to the main gully. This leads, with one steep short pitch to easy slopes.

Elliot's Downfall   115m   VII,5***
D. Cuthbertson   February 1979
The gigantic icicle (prone to collapse) below No.5 Gully gives an extremely steep and serious lead. Two easier pitches then lead to No.5 Gully.

No.6 Gully   240m   III/IV***
D. Munro and P. Smith   30th March 1951
The long gully on the right side of the face usually gives about four good pitches, the last one being the crux. A popular climb, recommended but the rock below middle ledge is very poor for belays and snow anchors will be necessary. A quick descent can be made by climbing up right via a chimney, 50m after the crux pitch to a series of ledges which lead right above steep ground and descend into Stob Coire nam Beith opposite Deep-Cut Chimney.

Chaos Chimney   135m   II/III*
A. Fyffe, E. Vveash, B. Jenkins, P. Hardman and J. Snodgrass   February 1969
The chimney gully going slightly right from the foot of No.6 Gully can be difficult in a poor build-up. Generally it offers three short sections.
154

Squaddie's Climb   130m   III
P. Moores and party   February 1980
An ice-flow often forms on the ground to the right of Chaos Chimney giving unserious practice in front pointing. The belays are however poor.

CLIMBS ON THE NORTH FACE OF AONACH DUBH

The face is dominated by the huge dark recess of Ossian's Cave. The cave itself is situated above a terrace, Sloping Shelf, which slants up from left to right and starts at the apex of the approach triangle. The right leg of this approach triangle is formed by a gully containing many waterfalls and lying to the left of the vegetatious terrace walls which rise from the floor of the glen to Ossian's Cave. The left leg is a slanting grassy ramp topped by cliffs which are split by a huge Y-shaped gully, Ossian's Close. The main climbs lie on either side of Ossian's Close but to the left of Ossian's Cave. The path up the right side of the triangle is often icy, so the recommended approach is along the grassy ramp (as the climbs are described) after crossing the River Coe as for the direct walk into Stob Coire nan Lochan.

To the left of Ossian's Close is a broad corridor which slants up right into the top of the gully. The icefall of Findlay's Rise starts at the foot of this corridor and rises on the left wall.

The steep and grassy nature of the approaches to all of the climbs provide a potentially dangerous base for avalanches after heavy snow falls or during thaw conditions.

Darwin's Dihedral   240m   VII,6/7***
D. Cuthbertson and M. Lawrence   28th December 1981
Towards the left end of the cliffs is a Y-shaped feature, obvious from the road. Climb the icefall beneath and the large right-facing branch of the corner which is to the left of the gully of Venom.

Divergence   170m   IV
A. Nisbet, C. Murray and S. Taylor   21st January 1984
Climbs the left branch of Darwin's Dihedral avoiding the crux of that route. Take the buttress on the left of the ice to gain the higher basin and follow the deep chimney of the left branch.

Venom   240m   V,5/6**
A. McAllister, M. Duff, R. Anderson and D. Brown   January 1979

Start about 30m left of Findlay's Rise below a steep chimney in the initial buttress. Climb the long chimney to trees and move left to gain and climb the gully left of White Snake. To the left of the initial pitch is a less obvious chimney which can be taken as a direct start to the main gully (**Viper Start** IV/V** *R. Anderson and D. Brown February 1979*).

King Cobra   280m   V/VI
M. Duff and R. Nowack   17th February 1986
Take the Viper start to Venom (120m). Ascend the chimney/gully to a point where an ice seep is seen on the steep left wall (25m). Climb the seep to a stance beneath the roof and right of icicles (35m). Traverse left to an icicle which is climbed, followed by a left-trending ramp then a steep groove to a block belay (60m). Easier ice to the top (40m).

White Snake   240m   IV**
R. Anderson, A. McAllister, D. Brown and M. Duff   January 1979
Climb the icefall just to the left of Findlay's Rise to a cave formed by a huge block. Follow a left slanting ramp then more easily up a gully to a roof. Traverse left to avoid the roof, regain the gully and continue to the top.

Findlay's Rise   240m   IV/V**
I. Nicholson and party   1978
Start at the icefall at the foot of the left wall of the corridor. A fine water-ice climb. Move steeply left onto the foot of the ice and climb less steeply to a small cave and belay. A long pitch leads to the top of the icefall from where mixed ground gives access to the summit.

Two Shakes   250m   III
M. Duff and A. Greig   24th January 1984
The buttress right of Findlay's Rise.

Ossian's Close   240m   III*
H. MacInnes and C. Williamson   February 1979
Above and slightly to the left of the apex of the approach triangle is a huge Y-gully. An unusual route, not as hard as it looks. Climb above the path to gain the gully at 15m. Easy ground leads to an ice wall going left to a cave. The upper section of the gully is gained by a through route leading to an easy exit.

AONACH DUBH NORTH FACE

1. DARWIN'S DIHEDRAL
2. DIVERGENCE
3. VENOM
4. VENOM - VIPER START
5. KING COBRA
6. WHITE SNAKE
7. FINDLAY'S RISE
8. MIDNIGHT SPECIAL
9. MIDNIGHT COWBOY
10. SHADBOLT'S CHIMNEY
11. AGAINST ALL ODDS
12. FINGAL'S CHIMNEY
13. DEEP GASH GULLY

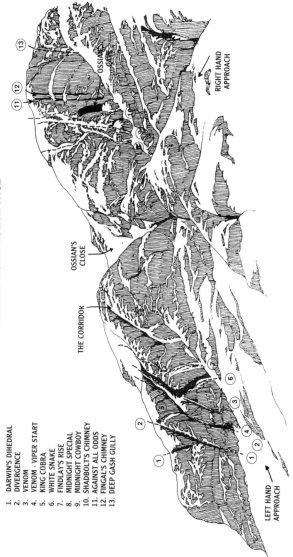

Midnight Special   300m   V,5*
I. Clough and K. Spence   1969
The prominent depression to the left of Ossian's Cave starting just up to the right from the apex of the approach triangle. From the bottom of the depression climb a steep pitch (crux) to reach a shallow gully. Climb this and bear left to reach the summit slopes or finish directly by the line of the depression.

Midnight Cowboy   370m   VI,5*
D. Knowles, Dud Knowles and W. Thomson   1974
Follows the line of an obvious gully running straight up, left of Shadbolt's Chimney. Start midway between Shadbolt's Chimney and Midnight Special. Follow iced walls and a chimney into the deepening gully which is followed with difficulty and poor protection to the top.

Shadbolt's Chimney   300m   V
D. and R. Goldie   13th February 1955
A deep chimney goes up from Sloping Shelf to the right of Midnight Cowboy start and not far below and to the left of Ossian's Cave. This gives the first 45m of the climb. The route then uses the grassy buttress on the right to avoid a loose section before a difficult 10m chimney leads on to an amphitheatre on the direct finish of Midnight Special. Finish up this. Rarely in condition.

Against All Odds   150m   VIII,8**
M. Fowler and C. Watts   14th February 1988
A prominent line right of Ossian's Cave and left of Fingal's Chimney. Start left of the weakness at a tree. Go up right and tension to a bendy sapling in the fault, then climb an overhang on tufts (?) to a niche and exit right to climb up to a nut belay (30m). Up a short wall on the right and the overhang above in the corner. Climb on tufts just right of the corner and gain a ramp coming in from the right, then continue to a belay ledge (30m). Climb on minimal ice smears and tufts right of the wide crack to beneath the overhanging section. On the first ascent three pegs were used to reach the next tufts leading steeply to snow. Gain a belay below a snow-filled chimney which slants up left (30m). Keep going in line with the lower pitches on minimal tufts and ice and protection to easier ground and a snow slope which ends 15m below Pleasant Terrace (45m). Follow a ramp on the left to Pleasant Terrace (15m). Either descend Pleasant Terrace or take easy slopes on the left.

Fingal's Chimney   190m   VII,7
W. Tauber and D. Gardner   1969

A fine sustained mixed climb requiring a lot of snow to be in good condition. One of the longest chimney climbs in the area. Very few ascents.

Right of Ossian's Cave are two narrow chimneys cutting the big wall. Climb the right-hand one. From the base of the chimney a series of ledges run down rightwards, terminating by a pinnacle. Start at the pinnacle and climb its right edge. A delicate traverse left beneath overhangs is made to a ramp which leads to the base of the chimney (45m). Climb the chimney in three long pitches to Pleasant Terrace. Either continue easily up the chimney or traverse left into Shadbolt's Chimney which can be followed to the top.

Pleasant Terrace   270m   III*
J. McArtney, I. Clough and party   4th January 1969

This climb and Deep-Gash Gully both start from the upper right-hand end of Sloping Shelf. The Shelf itself may give difficulty in icy conditions and the best route may be to cross the gully to gain the ridge on the right. Deep-Gash Gully is obvious immediately above the end of The Shelf. The entry pitches to gain the start of Pleasant Terrace proper start from a bay to the left of Deep-Gash Gully and consists of two pitches. The Terrace, which soon narrows to a thin and sensational ledge leads horizontally left for a long way.

After a slight descent the ledge broadens again below a deep chimney. Climb this with difficulty to the top.

Fall-Out   125m   VIII,7***
G. Taylor and R. Anderson   23rd January 1988

Start below the narrow chimney at the foot of Deep-Gash Gully and climb a corner and wall to belay just right of the chimney (30m). Climb the chimney to belay beneath a huge chockstone (25m), continue up the chimney to a ledge (25m). Move right along the ledge to another chimney (possible belay) which is climbed to the foot of a short chimney/ crack (40m). Move up then left to easier ground and back right to grooves, short walls and ledge (40m). Continue up left to easier ground.

Deep-Gash Gully   65m   IV
J. Cunningham and M. Noon   24th February 1957

This short gully at the top of Sloping Shelf can give a hard, technical problem but often banks out with snow.

Above Loch Achtriochtan is an impressive hanging garden of trees, heather and mosses. In the unusual event (in recent years) of a good long freeze at a low level the following three climbs might provide the exploring climber with good sport! Descend by traversing right at the high girdle ledge towards Dinner-time Buttress

North Face Route   600m   III
K. Spence and R. Anderson   *February 1982*
A central zig-zag line.

North West Face Route   450m   II
K. Spence and Co.   *1971*
Up the right side of the face.

Mr Softee   VII,6
M. Fowler and A. Saunders   *1983*
An isolated vertical icefall high on the face towards the left side.

CLIMBS FROM COIRE NAM BEITH

The magnificent northern corrie of Bidean is contained in the horseshoe ridges linking Stob Coire nan Lochan, Bidean nam Bian, Bidean's West Top, Stob Coire nam Beith and the nose of An-t-Sron. The main cliffs are the Diamond and Church Door Buttresses on the north face of Bidean nam Bian, the westward facing cliff on the flank of the north spur of the west top and the immense cliff cone leading to the summit of Stob Coire nam Beith.

    The main approach for this corrie starts from the road junction (GR 137566) through a gate immediately west of a road bridge spanning the River Coe. The path climbs steeply to the south and after about an hour levels off into a short gorge. At this point it is better to descend to the stream bed and follow either side of the stream uphill to avoid steep slabs below the deteriorating path. One will soon arrive at a stream junction. Straight ahead the left (east) bank of the main stream can be followed towards the col between Stob Coire nam Beith and An-t-Sron. From this col a steep but straightforward approach can be made to the summit of Stob Coire nam Beith: the west and main tops of Bidean. It also provides a good method of descent from all routes starting in this corrie.

A glance at the map (Sheet 41 - 1:50,000) will reveal three streams departing from the junction previously mentioned (GR 138554). If the vague central branch is followed it leads up into Summit Gully (described below). This stream approach can provide a good reference point for parties climbing on the complicated cliffs of Stob Coire nam Beith. The left-hand stream can also be followed in a south-easterly direction through a steep band of rock bluffs into the corrie beneath the cliffs. A waterfall will be encountered on this approach and is best avoided to the right (west).

The corrie continues up to a higher basin (often referred to as the Bidean Corrie) beneath the Church Door and Diamond Buttresses. Leading up steeply on either side of these two big buttresses are easy slopes to the cols between Stob Coire nan Lochan and Bidean, and between Bidean and the West Top. Both of these give descent routes but care should be exercised as they can become very icy. The right (west) of this upper basin is another subsidiary corrie which leads up between the cliffs of the West Top Spur and Stob Coire nam Beith, to a shallow col between the two summits. This gives another descent route although one should not glissade as there are a number of small rock outcrops in the corrie which may be hidden from above.

This route should be treated with care, especially if avalanche conditions prevail on north-facing slopes. In good conditions it is best to head well right in descent until an open snow slope is seen avoiding any cliffs.

AN-T-SRON (834m) GR 134548

This mountain lies up to the right of the main approach to Coire nam Beith. On the north side of An-t-Sron is the following climb.

The Chasm of An-t-Sron   360m   II/III
H.M. Brown, J. Matyssek, R.K. Graham and M. Smith   2nd January 1963
The great gully which splits the north face. The first pitch is normally turned but the other pitches higher up give good sport in icy conditions.

The following two climbs are on the east face of An-t-Sron (ie. the right wall of the subsidiary corrie between Stob Coire nam Beith and An-t-Sron). There are several easy gullies further right towards the mass of crags. The right-hand section includes a big prominent smooth slab. To the left of this is a snow bay at a slightly higher level from which rise steep twin diverging couloirs. These two obvious lines give the climbs.

Sac-O-Coal Couloir   150m   III
J. McArtney, D. Selby, B. Payne, J. Lines, and G. Drayton   18th February 1969
The left-hand line leads to a very steep and awkward corner exit before a final easy slope leads to the summit ridge.

Smashed Spectacles Gully   150m   II/III
I. Clough, F. Jones, R. Fox and C. Wood   18th February 1969
The right-hand line gives a short ice pitch in the first section and then follows a very steep chimney capped by an ice bulge before an easier continuation leads to the top.

STOB COIRE NAM BEITH (1,107m) GR 139545

The climbing on this mountain offers length, quality and variety. It will test the ability to find a route without a detailed description, especially higher up the climbs where many different options will be found. A fine peak for middle grade mountaineering routes.

The base of this massive and complicated cone of cliffs swings through a great arc so that all the climbs cannot be seen from the junction of the stream on the approach route. The most obvious feature here is the long Summit Gully. The slabby 90m Pyramid and (above and left of it) the bigger and steeper Sphinx Buttress form an indefinite ridge which bounds Summit Gully on the left. To the left of these is the region where the vague North-West Gully winds its way through the broken rocks of No.4 Buttress. The topography of the important central section can be seen in the diagram - the unmistakable Deep-Cut Chimney, the rightward-slanting ramp gully start of No.4 Buttress, the chimney-groove line of Crack Climb and the long shallow ice course of Central Gully. Beyond Central Gully the cliffs on the left-hand side of the cone fall back and eventually form a very big bay. Arch Gully runs up the right-hand side of the bay and to the left of the lower part of this is a big rock rognon split by a narrow chimney line, the start of the so-called No.1 Buttress. Above this rognon is a broad sloping snow shelf and the continuation of the No.1 Buttress chimney-line which leads up the rocks at the back of the bay. A shallow gully curls up and round the left-hand side of the rognon to the snow shelf. This is the approach to Broken Gully which has two forks, and lies in the left-hand recess of the bay. It leads up to the left to emerge on a shoulder. Beyond Broken Gully the final bold projection below the shoulder is called Zero Buttress.

The Corridors   160m   III/IV*
I. Clough, M.A. Hudson, C. Hutchinson, C. Williamson and D. Davies 12th February 1969
To the left of Broken Gully the face of Zero Buttress is cut by two shallow square-cut gully sections; the first ending at a ledge about 45m up and the other starting from this ledge a little further to the right and leading to the top of the buttress. This gives the line of the climb. The first corridor is often only filled with powder snow so a better alternative is to take the ice ribbon leading directly up the lower slabs to the second corridor. This should then give a couple of steep pitches leading to easier ground.

Broken Gully   160m   II
Mr & Mrs I. Clough 13th January 1966
The gully goes left up into the recess above the broad terrace which splits No.1 Buttress into two tiers. After about 30m a shallow gully on the right is followed until an easy leftwards traverse leads to the top of Zero Buttress. The left fork is a direct continuation and is separated from the normal route by a rock rib. It is steeper and holds more ice (Grade II/III).

No.1 Buttress   270m   II/III*
I. Clough and party 9th March 1967
The chimney line up the rognon left of Arch Gully and upper tier above gives a series of short ice pitches leading to the shoulder on Arch Gully.

Arch Gully   270m   II/III*
C.M. Allen and J.H.B. Bell December 1933
To the left of Central Gully is a shorter buttress, No.1 Buttress; dividing the two is Arch Gully. The first section is generally banked up and leads to a couple of steep pitches which are climbed direct to a shoulder. Continue to the summit or traverse off to the left.

Central Gully   450m   III/IV**
J. Clarkson and J. Waddell 12th January 1958
To the left of Crack Climb an ice-trap can form. Climb the ice-trap and follow the gully above past 3 to 4 steep pitches to easier ground. A fine climb.

Centre Route   450m   II/III
J.G. Parish, D. Haworth and D. McIntyre   February 1945
A rather indefinite climb starting round to the left of the lowest rocks to
the right of Central Gully. Zig-zag up the buttress for the initial 90m
until the angle lessens.

Crack Climb   450m   III
L.S. Lovat and N. Harthill   12th January 1958
Follows the obvious chimney-groove on the projecting side wall to the
left of Deep-Cut Chimney, starting about 25m up. The line leads to the
foot of a steep 10m wall which may be hard but escape to the right is
possible into the amphitheatre of Deep-Cut Chimney.

Deep-Cut Chimney   450m   III/IV***
W.M. MacKenzie and W.H. Murray   April 1939
The obvious deep narrow gully starting just to the left of the slanting
ramp is a classic climb. The lower part gives 2 or 3 steep pitches leading
at 130m to a small amphitheatre from where escape right is possible. Go
up left from the amphitheatre over iced rocks to a long steep crack line
which leads to easier ground. A further 200m to the summit.

No.4 Buttress   450m   II
The indefinite crest to the left of North-West Gully starting from the top
of the slanting ramp.

North-West Gully   500m   II*
Glover and Worsdell   April 1906
Sometimes mistaken for Summit Gully to its right but distinguished by
its lack of real entry and by a ramp cutting in from the left below No.4
Buttress. Open to considerable variation. The best start is by the slanting
ramp but steep and harder direct entries can be used. Easy snow then
leads to a fork. The left branch lacks interest so go right to another fork
amid impressive scenery. From here go to a shoulder from where a
steep wall leads to easier ground.

Cleftweave   450m   II/III
B. Clarke and A. Strachan   January 1972
Well to the right of North-West Gully, follow a series of gullies which
wind up left of the Pyramid to overlook Summit Gully. A steep short ice

STOB COIRE NAM BEITH NORTH FACE

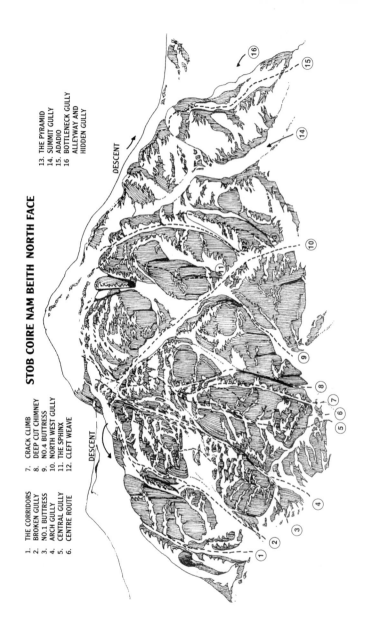

1. THE CORRIDORS
2. BROKEN GULLY
3. NO.1 BUTTRESS
4. ARCH GULLY
5. CENTRAL GULLY
6. CENTRE ROUTE

7. CRACK CLIMB
8. DEEP CUT CHIMNEY
9. NO.4 BUTTRESS
10. NORTH WEST GULLY
11. THE SPHINX
12. CLEFT WEAVE

13. THE PYRAMID
14. SUMMIT GULLY
15. ADADIO
16. BOTTLENECK GULLY
    ALLEYWAY AND
    HIDDEN GULLY

DESCENT

DESCENT

wall on the left is followed to gullies and a snow bowl. Follow a gully and ice pitch on the right to exit on summit slopes.

The Sphinx   135m   III/IV**
J. R. Marshall and I. Douglas   12th January 1958
Climb North West Gully until below a long black cave about half-way up. Start below and left of this cave by a shattered wall and climb to a small basin below the cave. Go right to a platform under the steep upper rocks. Climb high-stepped walls to reach the obvious chimney above (20m) and gain a tiny recess 3m up to the right. Grasp the top edge of a pinnacle-flake on the right-hand side, swing into space and start climbing for the top (75m), sustained!!

The Pyramid   90m   III*
J.R. Marshall and I. Douglas   12th January 1958
Begin at the lowest rocks above the start of North West Gully and follow the north ridge to the top.

On the right side of North-West Gully are two buttresses, one above the other. These form a ridge on the left of Summit Gully. The wedge-like lower buttress is **The Pyramid** and above is **The Sphinx**. Immediately left of and higher than The Sphinx is the steep column of **The Mummy**.

Summit Gully   500m   I/II**
The great long gully which starts just to the left of the lowest rocks of the Stob Coire nam Beith cone of cliffs. This route is often mistaken for North-West Gully. If snow has obliterated the vague stream bed mentioned in the earlier approach description look for the most obvious and continuous gully line of least resistance descending from just right (west) of the summit. This is well seen from the stream junction of the approach route. The route is generally straightforward with a possibility of ice steps to start with. A large cave pitch at mid-height might be impossible but can be turned by a right-hand gully branch 50m lower down. Above the cave it is straightforward to the exit which is just right of the summit cairn.

Adagio   400m   IV*
H. MacInnes, R. Birch, D. Chen, P. Judge and R. O'Shea   5th March 1969
Climbs the obvious narrow and steep gully in the crest of West Buttress which lies to the right of Summit Gully. Easily to a steepening with a

thinly iced left wall. Ascend the corner on the right followed by a left-rising traverse round the corner to twin icy chimneys. The left-hand chimney is climbed for 6m, then the right-hand one above a bulge and onto easier ground. Follow the main gully keeping left and climbing a cave direct towards the easier ground on the ridge to the right of Summit Gully.

The following three climbs lie on the left (east) wall of the subsidiary upper corrie between Stob Coire nam Beith and An-t-Sron. To reach these climbs follow the left bank of the stream (gorge) towards the An-t-Sron/Stob Coire nam Beith col, until above a large rock island. Hidden Gully is the obvious gully lying across to the left while Bootneck Gully is 75m higher up.

Bootneck Gully   245m   III
H. MacInnes, I. Duckworth, P. Wells, R. Ward and J. Parsons   March 1969
Take the central chimney line for two pitches until a steep ice wall has to be climbed. Above are easy slopes.

Alleyway   105m   III*
K.V. Crocket, D. Jenkins, C. Forrest and J. McEwan   23rd March 1969
The left-slanting gully right of Hidden Gully which can be used as an alternative start to that route. Mixed ground (30m) followed by easy snow leads to a very narrow alley capped by a large chockstone. From the top of the alley descend 10m into Hidden Gully below the difficulties.

Hidden Gully   245m   III/IV**
L. Lovat and W. Greaves   13th February 1955
Climb snow to a cave and exit to easy ground via the left wall. Continue past another cave to a narrowing with two exits, either of which can be taken to the ridge above.

THE WEST TOP OF BIDEAN NAM BIAN

Slightly higher up the corrie, these cliffs are on the western flank of the spur that descends northwards into Coire nam Beith from the West Top (ie. the highest point of the ridge between the summits of Bidean and Stob Coire nam Beith).

Closer   75m   IV**

C. Dale, A. Kassyk and D. Talbot   18th February 1982

Starts some distance below The Gash beyond broken ground. A prominent steep chimney with an icefall beneath it. Climb the icefall, chimney, bulges and chockstones to the top.

The Gash   120m   III/IV**

I. Clough, M. Hadley and M. Large   22nd March 1959

The steep cliffs below Hourglass Gully are split by a narrow, deep cleft gully gained by a rising traverse leftwards from Hourglass Gully or it may be reached directly. This gives a series of short bulging pitches barred at the top by a chockstone. Climb this on the left to a cave below a second huge chockstone. An intriguing through-route should be possible.

The Hash   125m   III

H. MacInnes and A.N. Other   February 1971

The obvious narrow gully to the right of The Gash formerly known as Caradhras Cleft. Start as for The Gash and gain the gully direct or move in from Hourglass Gully. Follow the gully to the top with a bulge where it narrows.

Hourglass Gully   120m   I

I. Clough and party   February 1966

The long tapering gully right of The Gash which opens into a snow fan near the top. Steep but straightforward.

Dubiety   110m   IV*

F. Yeoman and J. Mathie   23rd February 1987

An obvious line on the steep right-hand wall of Hourglass Gully. Start 30m up the gully and climb the steep iced corner-chimney to finish on the summit.

Minute Man   120m   IV*

M. Hamilton and R. Anderson   February 1983

The obvious groove in the buttress, right of the foot of Hourglass Gully. Gain entry into the groove over a roof and follow it to the top.

BIDEAN NAM BIAN (1,150m) GR 143542

The summit cliffs of Bidean consist of two main buttresses divided by a gully, Central Gully. The right-hand buttress is called Church Door Buttress, the left-hand one Diamond Buttress.

DIAMOND BUTTRESS

North Route   210m   II/III
J. Clarkson and F. King   6th February 1955
Skirts round the left end of the buttress following a series of chimneys and scoops which lead to a final rocky arête. Easy escapes are possible to the left. A slightly more difficult start (*Grade III, L.S. Lovat and W. Harrison March 1955*) is to follow an obvious steep scoop near but to the right of the normal route which leads to an arête on the right. The arête is followed by a traverse into another scoop and then the line goes up and left to join the normal route at about 80m.

Diamond Route   255m   VI,7
D. Rubens and G. Cohen   9th February 1986
Start in a bay midway between the toe of the buttress and Collie's Pinnacle. Gain the left-trending ramp and follow it and go further left (40m). Climb steeply to belay below a short V-chimney (30m). Avoid the chimney awkwardly to the right and go straight up, continuing to the upper girdle ledge (65m). Go right to the end of the ledge (60m). Climb a short difficult chimney to an arête and then to the top (60m).

Winter Route   250m   VII,7
K. Spence and J. McKenzie   February 1983
Start in a bay midway between the toe of the buttress and Collie's Pinnacle at a left-trending ramp. Climb the ramp for 10m until it is possible to break up right on steep mixed ground to a snow slope which is climbed to a rock wall. Go left and descend a little way, then climb slabby ground to a corner at the foot of a snow basin. Break out right by a steep groove on the right wall to a belay. Easier ground leads to the middle ledge where a groove is climbed. Continue up a groove to gain the upper girdle on the left. Go 30m left to the foot of a short wall which is climbed up and left to easier ground. Continue leftwards to gain the ridge.

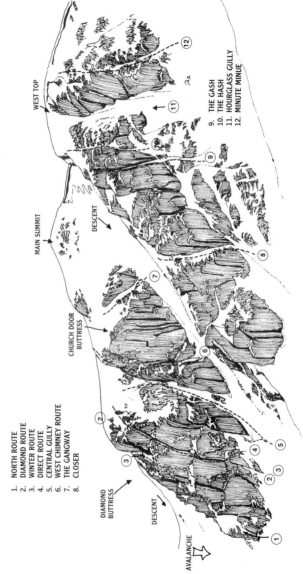

BIDEAN NAM BIAN

1. NORTH ROUTE
2. DIAMOND ROUTE
3. WINTER ROUTE
4. DIRECT ROUTE
5. CENTRAL GULLY
6. WEST CHIMNEY ROUTE
7. THE GANGWAY
8. CLOSER
9. THE GASH
10. THE HASH
11. HOURGLASS GULLY
12. MINUTE MINUE

WEST TOP

MAIN SUMMIT

DESCENT

CHURCH DOOR BUTTRESS

DIAMOND BUTTRESS

DESCENT

AVALANCHE

Direct Route   150m   V,6
M. Noon and J. MacLean   January 1959
Find a way up the central wall of the buttress to gain the right end of a long ledge which cuts across the face. Continue by grooves up and to the right to emerge on the right-hand ridge shortly below the summit. A solid coating of good snow/ice is essential for this route.

Central Gully   180m   I or II** (depending on the route followed)
A fine route but with some avalanche risk. Start to the right of Collie's Pinnacle and continue directly to the top up easy slopes. By taking a start to the left of the pinnacle and using the right fork near the top, a good climb of Grade II standard will be found.

CHURCH DOOR BUTTRESS

EAST FACE

Crypt Route　　　　　60m　　　IV***
H. MacInnes and party　February 1960
An unusual route winding its way through passages in the right wall of
Central Gully. Climb the first pitch of Central Gully and move right to
climb a steep chimney in the buttress. Where it closes step left and move
through the Crypt to emerge at the Arch, a platform above the initial
chimney. Finish as for West Chimney Route. Take a torch!

Flake Route　　　　　130m　　　IV**
G.R. Scott and F.W. Cope (Combined tactics)　18th March 1942
10m right of Crypt Route a huge flake is split from the buttress by a
crack. Climb the crack or ascend the other side of the flake by a traverse
around it 15m lower down the gully. From the col behind the flake go
up and right awkwardly then straight up broken ground until it is
possible to traverse left to the Arch. Cross the Arch and climb a shallow
chimney (crux) followed by grooves and walls to the top.

WEST FACE

West Chimney Route　　　180m　　　V,6**
A. Fyffe and H. MacInnes　8th February 1969
Up to the right of the lowest rocks of the buttress is a snowy bay leading
to an obvious deep chimney, which is followed past two difficult
chockstones to a cave where there is a through-route to the Crypt.
Beyond another chimney a ledge system leads left to the top of the Arch,
an airy platform formed by two huge jammed boulders. Above a hard
10m corner chimney the route continues up left to the summit.

The Gangway　　　　　70m　　　II
An obvious line high up on the right-hand wall of the buttress, slanting
up to the left to reach the top.

CLIMBS ON STOB COIRE NAN LOCHAN (1,115m) GR 148548

This magnificent peak dominates the view between Aonach Dubh and
Gearr Aonach. It is best seen to the south-west from a lay-by on the A82
(GR 168569) from where all approaches can start.

　　　The cliffs high in the north-east facing corrie immediately below the summit of Stob Coire nan Lochan usually give good winter climbing even when lower level cliffs are spoiled by thaw. The floor of the corrie is at about 800m and the cliffs, which have an average height of 165m are arranged in a semi-circle below the summit and the shoulder extending northwards from it.

Probably the most attractive approach is by the ridge of Gearr Aonach. After crossing the bridge below the Meeting of Three Waters (GR 173561) and following the track up towards Coire Gabhail (Lost Valley) as far as the beginning of the gorge section (about a half km above the bridge) the route cuts up to the right aiming for the cliffs of the East Face of Gearr Aonach some distance to the left of the Nose.

The route up the flank to the top of the Nose is known as the **Zig-Zags** (Grade I-II). Although marked by occasional cairns the route is not too easy to follow and it is wise to try and pick it out from well below. Careful inspection will reveal two obvious slanting terraces, up to the right and then back to the left winding up through otherwise sheer cliffs. The Zig-Zags are gained by walking leftwards up a grass slope below the cliffs until the start of the first terrace is reached in a corner immediately to the right of a 15m prow of rock. After about 30m of scrambling the terrace leads gently up to the right under some steep cliffs to an easy slope which is followed for another 30m or so before taking a short slab and gully corner on the left. This leads to a second big terrace which is followed to its left-hand end. After a short ascent, another long rightward rising traverse and a brief tack back to the left leads to a big cairn at the top of the Nose of Gearr Aonach. The ridge is then followed until an easy traverse can be made into the floor of the corrie (about $2^{1}/_{2}$ hours from the road).

This route is difficult to find in descent and, without prior knowledge and certainly in bad visibility, the valley route (next described) is preferable. Although it is not so attractive from the scenic point of view, the approach by the valley leading up between Gearr Aonach and Aonach Dubh is slightly faster than the previous route, more straightforward, and safer.

The bridge over the River Coe at GR 167566 is gained from a big lay-by on the south side of the road, east of Achtriochatan (GR 168569). A long steady ascent up the valley eventually leads over the final lip to the floor of the corrie (2 hours).

Another possible approach is by Dinner Time Buttress on the West Face of Aonach Dubh (described elsewhere). The topography of the corrie is relatively simple. Below the summit of Stob Coire nan Lochan is Summit Buttress. This name applies particularly to the steep right-hand face; the open face and broken rocks of the left flank can be climbed anywhere at Grade I standard. To the right of Summit Buttress are Broad Gully and Forked Gully. To the right again are the South, Central, North and Pinnacle buttresses, all separated by narrow gullies.

Boomerang Gully   210m   II*
J. Black, R.G. Donaldson and W.H. Murray   January 1949
This route curls round to the left of the steep rocks of Summit Buttress (and right of an indefinite rocky ridge which bounds the left flank) and swings back to finish by the ridge leading on from the top of the Buttress to the summit of the mountain. The first long tapering gully slope is followed up to the left from the foot of the steep rocks until an entry pitch on the right, rocky and frequently iced, leads up into the main couloir. If the entry pitch is missed the initial slope leads out onto the face of the left flank. The main couloir curves rightwards and leads to the final rocky arête.

Boomerang Arête   210m   III
J. Clarkson and R. Keltie   24th December 1956
Traverse right onto the buttress from the entry pitch of Boomerang Gully. Climb a short wall and grooves to a ledge. Turn the steep wall above on the right and the next steepening also by a chimney on the right which may form an ice pitch.

Ordinary Route   130m   V,6**
K. Spence & party   February 1971
Start just left of Scabbard Chimney and climb direct to a snow shelf then left to a corner. Follow the corner past a block and a snow shelf up left beneath the main buttress. An escape is possible into Boomerang Gully at this point. Ascend to the long, right trending groove and crack system and stepped ledges to the top. A harder variant (V**) is possible from the point where an escape can be made into Boomerang Gully by climbing an awkward short wall on the right which leads to a ledge system. Traverse the ledges rightwards including a mantelshelf to a higher step and sensational block belay. Sustained climbing of the tapering groove above then a short ramp and chimney, leads back left to easier ground *(M. Duff, N. Kekus, A. Nisbet 7th January 1986).*

STOB COIRE NAN LOCHAN
SUMMIT BUTTRESS

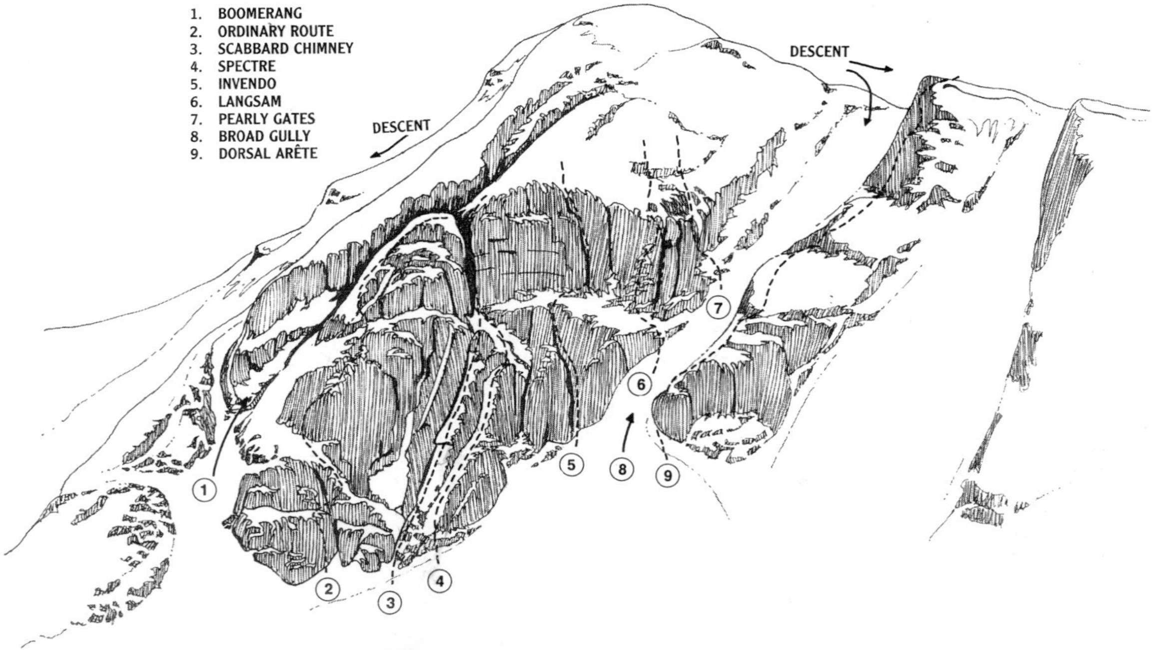

1. BOOMERANG
2. ORDINARY ROUTE
3. SCABBARD CHIMNEY
4. SPECTRE
5. INVENDO
6. LANGSAM
7. PEARLY GATES
8. BROAD GULLY
9. DORSAL ARÊTE

DESCENT

DESCENT

Scabbard Chimney 123m V,6
L.S. Lovat, J.R. Marshall and A.H. Hendry 12th February 1956
The obvious deep chimney which starts near the lowest rocks of the steep Summit Buttress and slants up to the right. The crux is a 'sentry box' at about 65m. Above the chimney, a gully on the left leads up to the final arête. A good plating of snow and ice is essential to make this climb feasible.

Spectre 120m IV**
K. Bryan and J. Simpson 12th January 1958
Follows a steep shelf 12m right of Scabbard Chimney. Ascend a broken wall until directly below the first true chimney of Scabbard (20m). Ascend a slab above and right to a ledge which is followed right to a point where an awkward descent gains the long shelf. Climb an icy bulge and groove followed by a steep slab and bulge to easier ground. Continue to a broad ledge and the narrow gully of Scabbard Chimney.

Innuendo 150m V,6**
H. MacInnes, R. Birch, P. Judge and R. O'Shea 1969
Starts above Broad Gully, opposite and level with the foot of Dorsal Arête, below an obvious chimney-groove which leads to a ledge cutting across the face. Climb the chimney-groove past a ledge (36m) into an overhung bay. Exit by a hard crack on the right wall and ascend more easily rightwards to a block belay below the upper wall. Traverse right beneath an overhung chimney until it is possible to climb steep cracks and gain the chimney by moving left above the overhanging section. Follow more easily up the chimney to the top.

Langsam 200m II**
H. MacInnes, M.C. MacInnes and party March 1969
Starts up the gully from Innuendo and follows the snow slope until under a rock wall.
Either: a) Traverse left on steep snow and up right to a short gully and the top.
or b) Climb a chimney on the right under the wall and continue the traverse up left to steeper snow then easier ground.

Pearly Gates 150m II/III
I. Clough and party 17th April 1966
Leaves Broad Bully at about half-height where the side walls of Summit

Buttress become more broken, and a notch is seen in the left-hand skyline. Zig-zag ramps lead up to this feature in 45m, and after passing through the 'notch' a shallow fan of snow leads directly to the summit.

Broad Gully   150m   I*
A very easy route which often provides the best means of descent into the corrie but care may be required in icy conditions.

Dorsal Arête   120m   II***
J. Black, T. Shepherd, J. Allingham and J. Bradburn   28th January 1951
Starting up a sprawling mass of rocks to the right of Broad Gully, the route becomes increasingly interesting as height is gained, finally tapering to a very narrow and well defined arête. Good rock belays, the climb is very useful in bad conditions.

Forked Gully   **Left Fork** 135m   I/II*
                              Right Fork   130m   II/III*
The gully to the right of Dorsal Arête gives a steep but normally straightforward snow climb by the Left Fork. The Right Fork (right of a 60m rock rib which splits the upper section) is steeper and often iced.

Twisting Grooves   130m   III/IV
W. Sproul and T. Carruthers   11th March 1962
Starts 30m to the left of Twisting Gully and follows a line of corners. Ascend the first corner to a small snow patch and continue up a crack topped by an overhanging chockstone (25m). Continue to a snow patch above the first pitch of Twisting Gully (30m) followed by snow to the bottom of a chimney (55m). The chimney leads to broken rocks near the top (20m).

Twisting Gully   150m   III***
W.H. Murray, D. Scott and J.C. Simpson   December 1946
One of the classic Scottish snow climbs. This route takes a shallow gully immediately to the left of South Buttress and is separated from Forked Gully by an indefinite rocky rib. The first 30m lead up into a deep recess from which there are two continuations. The normal route follows an icy chimney on the left until it bulges when a short left traverse is made across the gully wall to gain the left rib. There is an awkward mantelshelf move on the short arête which leads to easier ground. Above this crux pitch, about 30m of snow leads to another short ice pitch which can be

STOB COIRE NAN LOCHAN

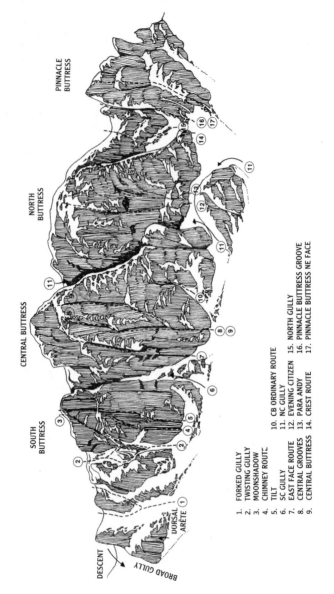

1. FORKED GULLY
2. TWISTING GULLY
3. MOONSHADOW
4. CHIMNEY ROUTE
5. TILT
6. SC GULLY
7. EAST FACE ROUTE
8. CENTRAL GROOVES
9. CENTRAL BUTTRESS
10. CB ORDINARY ROUTE
11. NC GULLY
12. EVENING CITIZEN
13. PARA ANDY
14. CREST ROUTE
15. NORTH GULLY
16. PINNACLE BUTTRESS GROOVE
17. PINNACLE BUTTRESS NE FACE

South and Central Buttress, Stob Coire Nan Lochan, Glen Coe

turned on the right if necessary (this pitch may even be completely obliterated). The gully continues without difficulty to the final wide fan and a choice of steep exits.

Twisting Gully Right Fork   150m   III*
J.R. Marshall and I.D. Haig   January 1958
A more difficult and more direct variation on the middle section of the normal route. From the deep recess, a very steep pitch up an ice corner is followed by a continuation runnel (separated from the original route by a broken rib) which joins the normal route below the final fan.

Moonshadow   150m   IV**
K. Crocket and C. Stead   January 1972
An interesting finish to the right fork of Twisting Gully. From the ice corner above the first main pitch, climb the right wall to a belay in a corner (36m). Climb this corner/groove past a chockstone to the top.

Chimney Route   125m   VI,7***
Start opposite the foot of Twisting Gully at the left end of a snow ledge. A good route often climbed in mistake for either **Direct Route** or **Tilt**. First ascent unknown. Climb steeply up the chimney (25m) then continue and go slightly right up turf to the left end of the upper terrace (45m). As for Tilt, a wall and a V-groove lead to the crest (25m), then easier to the top (30m). A variant is possible on pitch two by going straight up into the wide chimney of **Inclination**. This is separated from the upper terrace by a huge fin of rock.

Tilt   140m   VII,7***
M. Hamilton, K. Spence and A. Taylor   January 1980
A steep mixed climb with little ice and reasonable protection. To the right of Twisting Gully is South Buttress. This climb follows a very prominent chimney line just left of the blunt buttress crest. Follow iced cracks to the obvious chimney and groove (40m). Climb the groove till above an overhang. Move right with difficulty and climb a wall to belay on a large flake. Follow more grooves to a terrace and finish by a chimney and obvious V-groove on the left.

Inclination   145m   VIII,8***
R. Anderson, C. Anderson and R. Milne   17th February 1991
Belay at the start of Tilt. Move right to gain and climb a right-slanting,

stepped groove on the right side of the crest to a ledge and large block (20m). Climb the ramp on the left and carefully step up right onto a small block and climb cracks in the wall to a chimney. Climb the chimney and easier ground to join Tilt on the crest (20m). Climb up left onto the unlikely looking wall and finish up a short groove (20m). Ascend the wide fault above (Chimney Route), but go left up into a wide chimney whose right side is a huge fin of rock. Climb the chimney to belay on top of a boulder choke (45m). Move up left onto a chockstone, then right to easier ground and the top (40m).

S.C. Gully　　　　　　150m　　　III***

P.D. Baird, L. Clinton and F. Clinton　　March 1934

The steep gully between South and Central Buttresses is another classic and a serious route requiring good conditions. Early in the season a steep ice pitch often bars entry to the gully but, if it is too formidable, the rib on the left may give an easier alternative. Steep snow then leads up into the bed of the gully proper. The route then traverses up to the right to gain and follow a steep ice gangway which often has a bulge shortly before the top. A long run out will normally be required to reach a satisfactory belay above the pitch. Beyond this, steep snow leads to the cornice which may be quite difficult.

East Face Route 130m VI,7**

M. Hamilton and R. Anderson　　20th March 1982

On the east face of Central Buttress overlooking S.C. Gully are two parallel chimney systems. This route climbs part-way up the left-hand one before moving into the chimney on the right.

Climb the chimney and move left onto a pedestal (20m), then go back right and climb past the left end of a roof in the corner to belay in a shallow recess (15m). Gain the right-hand chimney system by difficult moves across the wall, around the arête, then up and right (30m). Follow the steep chimney to a belay on its left wall (45m). Go right to the crest and the finish of Ordinary Route (20m).

Central Grooves　　　　　120m　　　VIII,7***

K. Spence and J. McKenzie　February 1983

A well protected, hard mixed route. More difficult than Tilt. To the right of S.C. Gully is Central Buttress. The climb starts at the lowest rocks and follows an obvious groove just left of the crest throughout.

Central Buttress   135m   VIII,7***
K. Spence and M. Hamilton   12th February 1981
From a distance an elongated S-shaped crack can be seen starting from the foot of the buttress. This is the route. As for Central Grooves pitch one (30m). Traverse right climbing the wall to a corner which is followed to a ledge on the crest (20m). A short wall above is followed by easier ground right-wards to the edge. Go right and climb a pinnacle to a small snowfield (40m). Follow the chimney above before breaking out right below the top, and climb the last part of Ordinary Route (45m).

Central Buttress - Ordinary Route   150m   III***
H. Raeburn with Dr and Mrs C. Inglis-Clark   April 1907
Starts from the bay to the left of the lowest right-hand spur and goes up to the right to gain its crest. The ridge leads to a tower which is best turned on the right regaining the crest by a short chimney. A good route with splendid situations. N.B It is possible to by-pass the initial long pitch by a traverse in from the lower reaches of N.C. Gully. The first pitch is however very good!

N.C. Gully   155m   I/II**
The gully between Central and North Buttresses generally gives a steep but straightforward snow climb. Early in the season it may have short pitches. A good introductory gully.

On the right wall of **N.C. Gully** is an obvious tower with a roof at half-height which helps in locating the following three climbs.

Evening Citizen   95m   V**
K. Spence, H. MacInnes and A. Thompson   1971
Left of the roofed tower is a well-defined corner/chimney which gives the route to the crest.

Para Andy   90m   VII,7**
A Cunningham, A. Nesbit and A. Newton   8th January 1988
Climb the big corner/groove right of the roofed pillar. Climb direct to the groove (35m). Climb the groove until tight against a roof (loose), and traverse left to a mantelshelf. Belay ledge on the front face above the roof. Pass the short wall above to the left and back right to a crackline in the centre of the face which is climbed until possible to move left to a ledge and blocky arête leading to the top.

Intruder   100m   VII,7**
R. Anderson and G. Nicoll   14th February 1988
Climbs the slimmer right-hand groove right of the tower, starting at the
lowest rocks. Go up left passing Financial Times to the bottom of the
groove (15m). Ascend the groove with difficulty passing two pegs to a
flake, and continue to a ledge beneath the flake of Financial Times
(25m). Gain the groove on the left and climb it to the top of a pinnacle.
Go up, then right to climb a short groove then right to belay by a perched
block (35m). Easy to top (25m).

Financial Times   135m   IV*
R. Anderson and A. Taylor   19th February 1981
A line near the crest which starts at the lowest rocks. Gain then follow
a right-trending groove to a pedestal belay at large blocks (40m). Go up
and left to the edge, then up a flake crack to pull around to a ledge in the
centre of the face below a pinnacle (25m). Climb the large pinnacle
starting on its right (10m) and gain the groove of Intruder to the left
which is followed to the top (60m).

Crest Route   115m   IV***
R. Anderson and M. Hamilton   24th November 1985
To the right of N.C. Gully is North Buttress. This climb follows an
obvious groove just right of the buttress crest and starts at the lowest
rocks. It provides a good introduction to steep mixed climbing. Climb
broken stepped ground, a short wall and cracks to belay on a pedestal
(35m). Climb a flake crack above, and move right across a slab to gain
a corner which is followed to the crest. Step left at a large spike onto a
ledge (30m). Climb a flake crack above, and move right across a slab to
gain a corner which is followed to the crest. Step left at a large spike onto
a ledge (30m). Follow the groove and easy ground to the top, a short wall
is overcome by a stepped flake crack on the right.

North Face   90m   III
L.S. Lovat and K. Bryan   29th January 1956
The groove running up the right side of the buttress from the lowest
rocks. Go up and right to a snow ledge in North Gully, then climb to a
recess high up on the face. From the left end of a ledge climb a steep
groove and go left to a nose and easier ground.
N.B This route and those further right (Pinnacle Buttress) have a
disposition towards loose rock!

North Gully   75m   I/II

Divides North Buttress from Pinnacle Buttress. It is steep, sometimes gives a short pitch and often carries a heavy cornice.

Pinnacle Buttress Groove   60m   II/III*

L.S. Lovat and N.G. Harthill   5th January 1958

Follows a steep groove on the North Gully flank of Pinnacle Buttress to the left of a prominent arête. Start on the right near the foot of North Gully. An excellent short climb in icy conditions.

Pinnacle Buttress, North-East Face   90m   III

I. Clough and J.R. Woods   26th January 1967

Starts at the lowest rocks and climbs up right then left up a short groove to a steep wall. An icy corner crack on the right leads to a ledge and a higher ledge is gained up to the right. From the left end of this upper ledge an awkward chimney leads to the roof of the buttress.

To the right of Pinnacle Buttress are some short gullies and rocky outcrops which can provide good practice on a short day.

CLIMBS ON THE NORTH AND WEST FACES OF GEARR AONACH

The huge north face of Gearr Aonach dominates the ridge running between the Lost Valley and Stob Coire nan Lochan. The first two climbs described lie to the right side of this face while the remainder are situated on the steep buttress on the west face below the highest point of the ridge. All the climbs are easily reached from the path running up the east side of the stream on the approach to Stob Coire nan Lochan.

Avalanche Gully   300m   II/III*

H. MacInnes and party   1960

After crossing the bridge over the River Coe the main path strikes up towards the north face of Gearr Aonach before veering up to the right. The lower stream way of this gully crosses the path at this point. In hard weather conditions, the lower part gives a series of short water ice pitches. The gully follows a rightward slant and leads to the summit of the Nose. Take the right forks at the lower and upper branches. The Lower Left Branch is short, steep and interesting (Grade IV). The upper left fork when in condition is Grade IV.

Farewell Gully   150m   II/III
J. McArtney and party   February 1969
From slightly higher up the path from Avalanche Gully, the climb goes up in a direct line to meet the finish of that route. Several short pitches, but little of interest.

The following four climbs are on the buttress below the highest point of the Gearr Aonach ridge. Although short they have the attraction of easy access. The best approach is to follow the Stob Coire nan Lochan path till it passes a natural overhung shelter (1hr). The gully to the right of this welcome spot drains from the vicinity of the routes. The climbs described are really various finishes to the approach gully and are described from left to right.

Ciotach Route   90m   II/III
H. MacInnes and party   January 1959
This lies higher up the access gully on the left and climbs an icy section to the ridge with variations possible.

Rescue Team Gully   85m   II/III*
H. MacInnes and party   March 1966
The left-hand branch is a steep icy chimney with a through-route chockstone at its foot. Two good pitches.

Jim's Gully   106m   II/III
J. McArtney and party   March 1968
The central branch emits an icefall landing near the start of the previous route. Above this icefall the gully is easy.

999   135m   III**
H. MacInnes and party   February 1969
The right-hand branch gives a series of enjoyable short steep pitches. Follow the most obvious line.

North Face of Gearr Aonach
The following three climbs lie on the area left of the imposing rock nose of Gear Aonach which faces the road. They have the attraction of a short approach and quick descent.

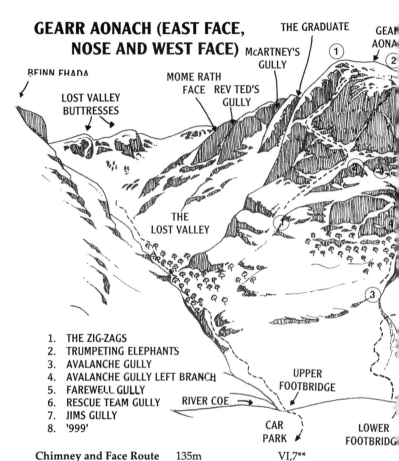

GEARR AONACH (EAST FACE, NOSE AND WEST FACE)

THE GRADUATE

GEAR AONA

McARTNEY'S GULLY

BEINN FHADA

MOME RATH FACE   REV TED'S GULLY

LOST VALLEY BUTTRESSES

THE LOST VALLEY

1. THE ZIG-ZAGS
2. TRUMPETING ELEPHANTS
3. AVALANCHE GULLY
4. AVALANCHE GULLY LEFT BRANCH
5. FAREWELL GULLY
6. RESCUE TEAM GULLY
7. JIMS GULLY
8. '999'

UPPER FOOTBRIDGE

RIVER COE →

CAR PARK

LOWER FOOTBRIDG

Chimney and Face Route   135m   VI,7**

R. Anderson, R. Milne and J. Naismith 7th February 1988

Start in the shallow gully between the main cliff and the vegetated ground to the left. Move up beneath a huge roof then go left to a ledge around an edge. Go steeply up vegetated ground, left then right to belay below a recess (35m). Climb right over a rib to a thin chimney which is climbed past a constriction to a belay (45m). 20m up the chimney to a ledge. Move left and follow the right-trending groove above to a bulge. Move up right past a tiny tree then left to easier ground above the fault.

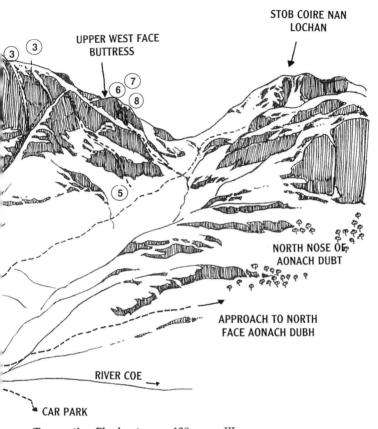

STOB COIRE NAN LOCHAN

UPPER WEST FACE BUTTRESS

NORTH NOSE OF AONACH DUBT

APPROACH TO NORTH FACE AONACH DUBH

RIVER COE

CAR PARK

Trumpeting Elephants   130m   III
M. Duff, I. McLeod and A. Owen   10th February 1988
Start as for White Rhino (next route) and follow the recessed chimney line.

White Rhino   150m   V
A. Cave and M. Duff   February 1988
From the end of the first right trending rake of the 'Zig-Zags', walk right
along a ledge to small chimney and tree in an exposed position. Climb
a very obvious diagonal rake for two pitches. Go into the gully above

(steep) to a recess below overhangs. Move steeply left with difficulty and climb ice covered slabs and grooves to easier ground and the 'Zig-Zags' descent.

N.B. The name of this route relates to the avalanche which was seen on the descent (top of 'Zig-Zags') after the first ascent!

CLIMBS FROM COIRE GABHAIL (Grid Square 1655)
(The Lost Valley)

Starting from lay-bys on either the north or south side of the road a path leads down to the footbridge over the River Coe near the Meeting of Three Waters (GR 173564). It continues up into the corrie, first through a gorge and eventually crossing the stream and passing through a boulder field to reach the floor of the corrie, a flat 500m of shingle and grass (45 minutes). The walk so far is very interesting and worthwhile for its own sake on an off-day. At the entrance to the corrie floor is the 10m Boulder - a useful landmark. Beyond the corrie floor there are two paths to the right of the stream and at different levels. The highest is the better of the two and makes a gradual ascent along the side of the valley until the stream is crossed above its deep gorge bed (accidents often occur here). The track disappears soon above this point and the two main approach/descent routes bifurcate. One route continues straight ahead to the col at the end of the valley - between Stob Coire Sgreamhach, 1,070m on the left and Bidean nam Bian. The slope is easy but there may be fairly large cornices. The other route bears up right into a subsidiary corrie which leads up to the col between Bidean and Stob Coire nan Lochan. Either of these are good descents but care may be required near the cornices. The cliffs of Stob Coire nan Lochan may also be reached by bearing back in a northerly direction, beyond the cliffs of the Upper East Face of Gearr Aonach, obliquely across the hillside to reach the shoulder where the Gearr Aonach ridge rises steeply towards the summit of Stob Coire nan Lochan.

LOST VALLEY ICE SLABS

On the east side of the stream emerging from the boulder field below the flat part of the Lost Valley are tiers of slabby wet rock that quickly freeze in a cold winter. Several good pitches have been made on these, steep slabs. The steepest central icefall hereabouts is **Bop Till You Drop,** IV 105m *(M. Garthwaite and A. Foster 6th December 1981).* Various trees can be used for belays and abseil points.

BEINN FHADA (GS 1654) AND STOB COIRE SGREAMHACH (GS 1553)

These two peaks link a fine ridge crest and form the steep slopes which enclose Coire Gabhail to the south-east. The ridge is steep and rocky on all sides and gained most easily from the east below point 811m (GR 172553). Ascent to this point is also possible from Coire Gabhail, starting up the steep and tedious slope 200m beyond the large 10m Boulder. Take the line of least resistance and arrive at a bealach after 1-1$^{1}/_{2}$ hours of upward toil! The ridge is followed with continual interest to a rocky step (GR 157538), which should be turned on the left before ascending to the summit of Stob Coire Sgreamhach. This fine outing is similar in parts to the Aonach Eagach (Grade II). In descent the easiest route is via the bealach at GR 151537. Care should be taken on this slope. The cornice can be large and the avalanche potential considerable at certain times.

The north face of Stob Coire Sgreamhach provides long and interesting approaches to the summit at Grade II depending on the line you take. Access to this face is best by the track up the west bank of Allt Coire Gabhail as far as the stream junction beyond the gorge (GR 154543). From here, strike up the steepening slope to the south beneath the summit cone.

EAST FACE OF GEARR AONACH

These climbs are all on the right-hand side of Coire Gabhail beyond the Lost Valley Boulder. Particularly useful when conditions are poor at higher levels and for their relatively short approach. However, many of them are fine climbs in their own right and some rank with the best in Glen Coe. Icy conditions are preferable. The best descent is by the Zig-Zags (if the team is competent and the visibility good) on the Nose of Gearr Aonach (described under Stob Coire nan Lochan) but most people prefer to walk towards Stob Coire nan Lochan and descend into the upper part of the Lost Valley or Coire nan Lochan. The routes are described from left to right and climbers new to the area should try and locate the more obvious gullies of Ingrid's Folly and Rev Ted's as useful reference points when exiting from the gorge section of the approach walk onto the flat area below the climbs.

Gully C   230m   I
Probably G.S.W.C. parties
A long shallow couloir on the extreme left before the cliffs fade out
entirely. It may contain a few short pitches. Competent climbers may
find this route useful as an approach to Stob Coire nan Lochan.

Gully B   230m   II
Probably G.S.W.C. parties
The next gully to the left of Gully A is straightforward except for one
large chockstone pitch.

Gully A (Left Branch)   235m   IV
H. MacInnes and G.S.W.C. party   February 1970
This is the branch of the gully which starts as a very steep ice pitch
slightly to the left of the main Gully A. Follow the gully line throughout
(escape possible halfway up on the left) and take either the chimney line
above or break out right up steep iced rock.

Gully A (Central Branch)   230m   IV
D. Haston and J. Stenhouse   January 1969
Gully A divides at the start of the main pitch and this variation takes a
line directly up a steep ice scoop.

Gully A   235m   III/IV
H. MacInnes and D. Crabbe   January 1964
Starting some distance beyond where the path rises from the floor of the
Lost Valley. It runs the full height of the face, is indefinite in its lower
part, deep cut in the middle and becomes a steep straightforward slope
in the upper section. It faces south and is hidden until immediately
below it. A pitch climbed on the left leads into the gully which is
followed to the right to a bulging groove, the crux of the climb.

Lost Leeper Gully   300m   III
H. MacInnes and G.S.W.C. party   13th February 1969
The shallow indefinite gully which comes down immediately to the left
of the Mome Rath Face and reaches the lower slopes of the valley above
the gradually rising path. The route weaves its way up through the
lower crags, giving interesting route-finding, and the more distinct
upper gully should give at least two good ice pitches. The belays in the
main part of the gully are poor.

EAST FACE OF GEAR AONACH

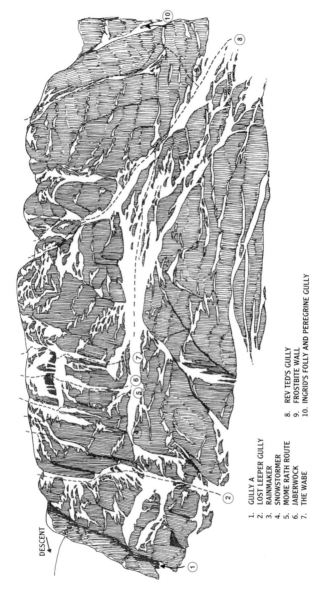

1. GULLY A
2. LOST LEEPER GULLY
3. RAINMAKER
4. SNOWSTORMER
5. MOME RATH ROUTE
6. JABERWOCK
7. THE WABE

8. REV TED'S GULLY
9. FROSTBITE WALL
10. INGRID'S FOLLY AND PEREGRINE GULLY

DESCENT

Given the right conditions the upper cliffs to the left of Rev Ted's Gully give some of the most sensational ice climbing in Glen Coe. The terrace below the upper wall can be reached by the lower sections of Rev Ted's or Lost Leeper Gullies. The upper wall (Upper East or Mome Rath Face) has high up, a long barrier of overhangs. In hard conditions much of the face becomes masked with smears of ice and the overhang is decorated with a fantastic fringe of icicles which can attain 10/15m in length.

Rainmaker   100m   VI,5***
D. Cuthbertson and M. Duff   February 1980
At the left-hand end of the upper face, next to Lost Leeper Gully is a large ice-cased corner. Climb a long pitch up ice smears to the left of the corner and belay in a recess. Now climb the corner with a short excursion on the left wall.

Snowstormer   100m   VI,5/6***
D. Cuthbertson, A. Paul and C. McLean   January 1984
This route follows close to the exposed edge right of Rainmaker. Climb to a belay on a pedestal above an obvious V-notch (27m). Follow icy corners above to beneath the overlap overlooking the corner of Rainmaker, belay. The vertical corner of the second pitch is well protected. Easier climbing leads to the top.

Outgrabe Route   115m   V**
R. Anderson and R. Milne   January 1980
A direct start and variation finish to Mome Rath Face Route, creating a virtually independent line. Start 10m left of Mome Rath Face Route and climb directly to a gully/chimney fault which is climbed in two pitches, keeping left of the icicle fringe on the second pitch.

Newsholme's Groove   140m   V,5**
G. Hornby and C. Schaschke   February 1986
A broad groove between Mome Rath Route and Snowstormer, a bold line. Start at an open bay, move up right then left and climb a thin vertical step, belay. Follow the open groove above and move right along the icicle to finish up the last groove left of Mome Rath Route. Belays on ice screws may be necessary.

Mome Rath Face Route   135m   V,5***
A. Fyffe and J. McArtney   *16th February 1969*

The general line of the route is a long leftward slant. It starts below the icicle fringed overhang by an obvious broad ramp and continues the line up to the left into a chimney. This is followed for about 20m before going left again into another chimney which leads to a bay. A slabby ice plated rib on the left is followed by a short steep corner chimney. Again this route combines sustained technical climbing with a high degree of exposure.

Jaberwock   135m   VI,5**
A. Paul and D. Cuthbertson   January 1984
Climbs the obvious icefall between The Wabe and Mome Rath Route, taking in the ice fringe at the top.

The Wabe   135m   V,5***
I. Clough, H. MacInnes and J. Hardie   16th February 1969
Approximately follows the line of a prominent icefall to the right of the icicle fringe. A short wall is climbed. Belay on a snow ledge above the main terrace. The route then goes up slightly to the right before making a long diagonal leftward traverse across the icefall towards a prominent nose and a stance at 45m. After passing below the nose (immediately above an overhang) the route veers right then left to reach a pedestal stance below the right edge of the icicle fringe. Then move back right to climb the icefall where it passes through a recessed panel, good stance on the right above this section. The final pitch goes diagonally right and then back left. The route is sustained throughout and extremely exposed.

Whimsy   120m   IV**
R. Clothier and D. Hawthorn   January 1984
The icefall a few metres right of The Wabe.

Rev Ted's Gully   300m   II/III**
H. MacInnes and Rev Ted   February 1960
Follows the obvious long couloir which slants leftwards up the full length of the face. The lower pitches are usually straightforward and lead to an obvious junction in the upper cliffs. Several alternatives are available. The best is to follow an ice chimney line just to the left of the ice fall at the junction, or to take the icefall direct. If the easy right branch is followed another steep chimney line will be found leading up from a bay; interesting but awkward. From the same bay an easy escape right can be made, reducing the whole climb to Grade I/II.

Between Rev Ted's and Ingrid's Folly and Peregrine Gully, the cliffs of Gearr Aonach give broken crags in the lower half leading to an almost continuous wide horizontal terrace. Above the terrace are a series of steep walls, unpleasantly grassy in summer but which give good winter climbing. The first big break in these upper cliffs is a large rightward facing corner - McArtney Gully.

Frostbite Groove   200m   V,5
H. MacInnes and G.S.W.C. party   February 1969
At the point where Frostbite Wall traverses back across the obvious ledge, take the ice chimney/groove line up and slightly right. Break out left after one pitch, over ice bulge to gain ice scoop. Climb scoop and small chimney to the top.

Frostbite Wall   200m   V,5
H. MacInnes, A. Gilbert, P. Debbage, D. Layne-Joynt and D. Allright February 1969
Take the main line of the ice ribbon up the wall, gaining it first by a rightward traverse from the bottom of it, then back left to it some 50m up via a ledge. Climb the ice ribbon direct to the top.
N.B. This route is usually in condition when the ice ribbon is complete from top to bottom of the cliff.

McArtney Gully   175m   II/III
H. MacInnes and G.S.W.C. party   3rd February 1969
The lower half of this big corner gully is reasonably straightforward, but the upper part is very steep. A vertical chimney is followed to a diagonal groove and corner which gives the crux.

Ingrid's Folly and Peregrine Gully   300m   II*
G.S.W.C. party (Glencoe School of Winter Climbing)
The foot of Ingrid's Folly is only about 5 minutes walk diagonally up the slope to the west of the Lost Valley Boulder. It is a well defined gully tucked away in a corner, much better than its appearance might suggest. The long grassy buttress to its right (and immediately left of The Graduate) is John Gray's Buttress, Grade II. Ingrid's Folly consists of several relatively easy rock pitches which give good sport when veneered in ice. Above the last pitch, where the gully gives an easy slope to the top, a 100-metre traverse to the left leads into Peregrine Gully. This gives further pitches; another cave with a through-route and an

easy passage below a gigantic block which forms an archway just before the steep exit.

John Gray's Buttress   300m   II
H. MacInnes   January 1968
Follow the easiest line up the buttress just right of Ingrid's Folly. A good freeze is needed.

The Graduate   175m   III/IV
D.A. Knowles, J. Loxham, D. Wilson and A. Wilson   8th February 1969
The boulder field which blocks the entrance to the floor of the Lost Valley is the result of a great landslide which has left a huge deep recess in the cliff of Gearr Aonach. Follow the great right-angled corner at the left-hand side of this recess. It is most easily reached by going up and slightly rightwards from the Lost Valley Boulder. Rarely in condition.

Bunny's Route   95m   III*
I. Clough and C.G. Kynaston   29th March 1967
Not often in good condition this route can provide a fine outing with a short approach if avalanches are likely on higher cliffs. Starts about 50m up left of the lowest rocks just left of the 'Zig-Zags'. The main feature is a fault leading to a prominent chimney. Descent by the 'Zig-Zags'.

LOST VALLEY MINOR BUTTRESS

The smaller and left-hand of the two prominent buttresses at the head of the valley and below the middle of the ridge leading up from the col to Bidean. Routes are described from left to right.

Left-Hand Gullies   75m   I
To the left of the buttress are two easy gullies separated by a rocky rib.

Left Edge Route   76m   III
J. Moffat and C. Dale   February 1984
Start to the left of Chimney Route. Follow the obvious gangway up left to a short corner which is climbed to the top.

Chimney Route   75m   III/IV*
R. Marshall and J. Moriarty   January 1959
The obvious deep chimney to the left of the centre of the face. A series

of chockstone pitches can give considerable difficulty.

Minor Issue 80m V,6*
R. Anderson and G. Taylor 10th January 1988
Climbs the corner-groove line left of the buttress edge between Chimney Route and Central Scoop.

Central Scoop 85m III/IV
I. Clough and Mrs N. Clough February 1969
This is the chimney line between Chimney Route and Right Edge. The chimney (short) starts from a platform some 13m up and the route takes this corner/chimney, then follows the buttress to the top.

Right Edge 120m III/IV**
J.R. Marshall, J. Stenhouse and D. Haston February 1959
At the right-hand side of the face a broad snowfield-ramp leads up rightwards below overhangs. Access to the ramp is gained by an icy chimney below its left end and an arête leads from the top of the ramp to the summit.

Minor Adjustment 115m V,6**
R. Anderson and C. Greaves 19th February 1989
The obvious groove and corner just up the gully from Right Edge. A direct line which joins that route after its upper traverse. Climb the groove steeply to a small ledge and spike then go steeply left up a ramp around the edge to ledges. Traverse right back into the corner and belay higher up (45m). Climb the corner, move right and climb a short groove and step right below a small roof. Follow the snow ramp to a belay above a short wide crack (25m). Climb to the top (45m).

Right-Hand Gully 75m I
Probably G.S.W.C. parties
The gully immediately to the right of the buttress gives a straightforward but steep climb and often has a large cornice.

LOST VALLEY BUTTRESS

The large right-hand buttress is in two distinct sections; an easier angled left-hand portion but very steep and set back at a higher level on the right. The routes are described from left to right.

LOST VALLEY BUTTRESSES

1. LEFT EDGE ROUTE
2. CHIMNEY ROUTE
3. MINOR ISSUE
4. CENTRAL SCOOP
5. RIGHT EDGE
6. MINOR ADJUSTMENT
7. LEFT HAND GULLY
8. SABRE TOOTH
9. DIRECTOSAUR
10. PTERODACTYL
11. NEANDERTHAL
12 SAVAGE
13. BARRACUDA
14. RIGHT HAND GULLY

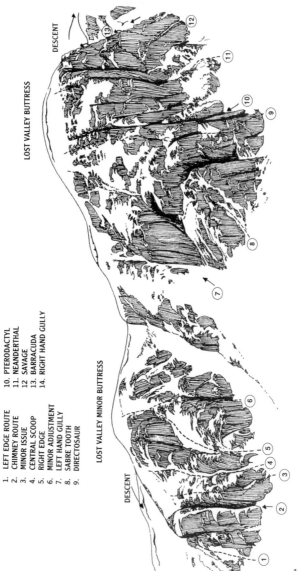

DESCENT

LOST VALLEY MINOR BUTTRESS

LOST VALLEY BUTTRESS

DESCENT

197

This cliff has been the venue for a number of hard mixed (torquing) routes of high quality in recent years. It should be remembered that this type of climbing is very different from the traditional winter ice climb which often consists of poorly protected leads on steep ice. Torquing (mixed) routes are often well protected with minimal icing.

Left-Hand Gully   90m   I
Probably G.S.W.C. parties
The gully is bounded on the left by a broken indefinite rib of rock. Straightforward climbing to a steep corniced exit.

Sabre Tooth   135m   III/IV**
I. Clough and H. MacInnes   9th February 1969
There is a prominent vertical 45m corner towards the right-hand side of the left-hand section of cliff. This has been climbed (**Delusion**) but gives a much more difficult start which would elevate the general standard of the climb to Grade IV/V.

      Starting to the left of the corner, the route goes up into a recess and breaks out rightwards, eventually arriving on a terrace above the big corner. The terrace leads back left to the foot of a steep shallow 15m corner (good belays on the left). The corner is hard for a climb of this standard but well protected. Above it, a line of grooves is followed to the top.

Directosaur   160m   VI,7**
G. Ettle, R. Anderson and R. Milne   March 1989
Start at the lowest rocks and climb the shallow groove just left of the edge. Go left and up to a ledge which leads back right to the edge. Climb a steep flake crack on the left and easier ground to below the corner of Tyrannosaur (45m). Climb the corner and grooves up the right side of a huge block-like feature to its top (30m). Go right and climb a short groove to regain the crest and snow grooves leading to the upper rocks and final slopes.

Tyrannosaur   150m   VI,7*
I. Clough, D. Morrish and E.S. Taylor   5th March 1969
Takes the well defined right edge of the left-hand area of the cliff. Starts on the right wall well below the corner of Pterodactyl and 10m up from the lowest rocks. Climb a shallow chimney and the thin continuation crack trending slightly left over the edge to a snow bay. Climb the steep

corner and grooves up the left side of a huge block like feature to easier grooves which lead to the top.

Pterodactyl (Moonlight Gully)   110m   V,5/6*
H. MacInnes and D. Crabbe   January 1964

Follows the line of the shallow gully lying in the corner which divides the two sections of cliff. The overhanging entry to the upper couloir is difficult but relatively short. The route follows a steep corner to a stance beneath the overhang which projects for 2m then climbs to gain the upper couloir using the crack to the left of the main icicle formation.

N.B. The central section of this route is climbed on aid and is out of character with the rest of the route. In years of good icing it may be possible to climb steep ice on the right of the central section. Chockstones have fallen out of this section.

Moonlighting   120m   V,7**
R. Anderson, G. Taylor and N. West   27th January 1988

An obvious line right of Pterodactyl at the top of the bay. Gain the groove and a ledge at the foot of a wall (35m). Move up the steep flakeline on the left and left at its top to the edge overlooking Pterodactyl, then move up right to a shallow groove which leads to a short wall (35m). Move into the gully of Pterodactyl which is followed to the top (50m).

Neanderthal   125m   VIII,7 *
R. Anderson and G. Nicholl   February 1987

An improbable-looking line up the huge corner, 30m right of Pterodactyl. Very good climbing according to those who have done it! A steep mixed climb.

Easily up gully and left wall to a platform (18m). Traverse right and climb chute to belay at a cul-de-sac (15m). Traverse right until possible to climb to the base of corner and a small ledge (21m). Follow corner to right side of a square roof. Move left underneath this and follow recessed wall above, towards an obvious narrow slot on the skyline (27m belay). Easier climbing soon leads to the top.

Savage   80m   VII,8**
G. Taylor and R. Anderson   31st January 1988

Climbs the obvious monolith on the wall right of Neanderthal, gained from the leftward ramp which starts at the edge of the buttress. Climb the ramp to a belay at the foot of the monolith (20m). Climb the corner-crack on the right side of the monolith with difficulty to a belay on its top (10m). Stepped walls and grooves are climbed above until forced into a traverse right around the buttress edge into a shallow groove. Climb the groove, then the rib just left of the steepening on Barracuda. Go right and finish on Barracuda (50m).

Barracuda   80m   V,7
R. Anderson and R. Milne   January 1988
Another steep and difficult mixed climb, although the easiest of the harder routes on this crag. Up the obvious steep crack line which springs from the left trending ramp line right of Neanderthal. Start at the edge of the buttress. Follow the ramp to a belay at the foot of the crack. Climb the crack (with very hard initial moves) to the buttress crest. Climb the gully above to the top.

Trilobite   60m   II/III
H. MacInnes and I. Clough   9th February 1969
On the side wall of the buttress, leaving the right-hand gully where it begins to narrow and opposite a ramp which goes up steeply out to the right, Trilobite follows a very steep groove which runs directly up the gully wall to the top of the buttress.

Right-Hand Gully   90m   I/II
Probably G.S.W.C. party
A steep gully with a big cornice, often containing a small ice pitch. About 30m up, below the steepening and narrowing to the pitch and level with the runnel of Trilobite, is a variation sloping steeply up to the right - **The Ramp** (Grade I/II).

Descent Gully   I
Separated from Right-Hand Gully by a rocky rib. Straightforward and usually corniced.

CLIMBS ON STOB DEARG (GR 223543)
BUACHAILLE ETIVE MOR (1,022m)

Buachaille Etive Mor is a long ridge with four tops. Stob Dearg is the north top, a beautifully symmetrical cone as seen from the junction of the roads leading down in to the glens of Etive and Coe. Of the four tops it is the highest and the only one which gives much climbing and it is generally referred to as The Buachaille.

The mountain is an excellent summer rock climbing area, whilst in winter its natural ridge and gully lines are amongst the best in Scotland. The view from the area surrounding Curved Ridge is one of the most striking panoramas of any British hill.

The most popular routes are all on the central section of the mountain above the waterslide slab, but many fine climbs can be found on the area overlooking Glen Etive between D Gully Buttress and The Chasm.

Many of the climbs start from the Crowberry Basin - below Crowberry Ridge and Gully.

The most usual starting point is from Altnafeadh (GR 222563) on the main road (parking available in several neighbouring lay-bys). The River Coupall is crossed by a bridge leading to Lagangarbh. Beyond the hut, a track leads south-eastwards, gradually rising, to cross the foot of Great Gully after about 1¹/₂kms. From this point one can take a shortcut by following the lower easy part of North Buttress and bearing left into the basin below Crowberry Ridge. Alternatively one can continue following the track below North Buttress, which rises slowly to meet the prominent **Waterslide Slab**. From this slab ascend straight up the steep and loose heather and scree slopes to its left. Higher up a delicate traverse right must be made above steep rocky ground in order to gain the foot of Crowberry Gully or Curved Ridge (1¹/₂ hours). Routes to the left (south) of D Gully Buttress can also be approached via the Glen Etive road.

For climbers new to this area it is advisable to drive along the main road towards the Kingshouse in order to view the main features of the mountain before choosing a route.

BEWARE! Many avalanche incidents have occurred in the Great Gully and Crowberry basin areas.

Descent

There is only one reasonable descent route in winter. From the summit follow the fairly level ridge for 300m bearing 250° Grid. Then change course to 270° Grid and descend to reach a shallow cairned col at the head of Coire na Tulaich (more usually called Lagangarbh Corrie). This section can be particularly difficult in white out conditions. There are occasional cairns but it may be necessary to stay roped up and take both front and back bearings to keep on course. The most common mistake is to continue too far south-west and descend into Glen Etive. This slope is not too difficult but it is a long walk back on the road. Care should be taken not to stray too far to the north too early as there are some large crags at the head of Coire na Tulaich. From the col a steep initial slope leads down into the corrie. This slope is often in a hard icy condition and it may be best to wear crampons and to belay. Even in soft conditions it is better not to glissade as there are often boulders and screes exposed lower down. There have been many accidents here. The lower part of the corrie (there is a track down the left-hand side) leads easily down to Lagangarbh and the road.

Also it is possible to ascend slightly from the col to point 903m (GR 214542) and descend north by the ridge to the west of Coire na Tulaich. All the large outcrops on this descent are avoidable by moving left and the ground is more interesting than Coire na Tulaich. The routes are described from left to right.

CLIMBS ON STOB DEARG FROM GLEN ETIVE
SOUTH EAST FACE

The area between Central Buttress and the Chasm is both complicated and huge in scale, requiring good judgement and climbing skills. No particular easy exits exist until the summit or Curved Ridge is reached. This section of the mountain is recommended to experienced climbers who savour the challenge of long routes with an 'Alpine' feel about them. Due to its south easterly aspect this part of the mountain often produces good neve when other cliffs are covered in powder. Snow conditions can change as height is gained and a wary eye should be kept for potential avalanches.

The Chasm   450m   III/IV
This route is approached from the Glen Etive road (GR 233531), $2^1/2$kms from the main road junction. At this point two streams can be seen on the map joining by the road, and The Chasm drains into the northmost one. It forms an obvious gulch on the hillside to the right (west), and is blessed with a short approach. During winters of heavy snowfall this climb may be straightforward. In leaner conditions several pitches will be present and the nature of the climb becomes hard and time-consuming. Several variations exist higher up the gully with the direct continuation being the most difficult. Escapes from the gully can be made at a number of points, most easily to the left.

The Chasm North Wall   360m   II*
J.H.B. Bell, J.W. McGregor, J. Napier, R.G. Napier   December 1895
Takes the rock walls bounding The Chasm on the right. Start 100m above the first pitches on The Chasm. Two steep buttresses are encountered.

The Chasm to Crowberry Traverse   1,000m   II*
Easily seen from the Glen Etive road this expedition starts at the edge of the Chasm below the first high wall of the previous route at an altitude of around 550m. An obvious feature is an undercut cave at the halfway mark. The line can be followed towards the top of Curved Ridge or harder more direct variants taken towards the summit. An excellent day out for explorers!!

Lady's Gully   240m   IV**
J.R. Marshall, I.D. Haig and G.J. Ritchie (Left Fork)
L.S. Lovat and W.J.R. Greaves (Right Fork)
Easily seen on the hillside to the west of stream junction (GR 240537), this gully is the first one north of The Chasm. Not often in good condition, but when it is (during winters of heavy snowfall and good build-up), the climbing is very good. Follow the line of the gully to a steep wall (45m). Climb the wall, which can be difficult (45m), and several more difficult pitches to a fork in the gully. The left fork is the best option. This leads to easier ground beneath the summit ridge. Finish either by gaining the summit or by traversing left above The Chasm and descending into Glen Etive. If the right fork is followed the top of Curved Ridge can be gained beneath Crowberry Tower.

Waterslide Gully   90m   IV**
T. McAulay & C. Murray   9th February 1986
Left of The Veil a shallow icy channel. Climb to a hanging stance (50m) then continue straight up (40m).

The Veil   180m   V,5**
T. Brindle & A. Moore   20th February 1986
Climb the icefall right of Waterslide Gully in two pitches. Another pitch up a snow bay leads to a vertical column of ice which is climbed to easier ground.

Right of the previous two climbs is the main mass of **Central Buttress**.

The right side forms a steep narrow buttress of rock and on the left it is bounded by the shallow Waterslide Gully. It is a two-tiered crag lying low down on the south east side of the mountain.

Direct Route   95m   IV*
T. McAulay & D. Sanderson   21st January 1984
This route lies on the south face of Central Buttress and is reached by traversing left under the lowest rocks of Central Buttress beneath a distinctive yellow cave and climbing up to a small pinnacle. Pass the pinnacle on the right or left and climb to a ledge which is followed up right to a 6 metre chimney which is followed to Heather Ledge. Descend from Heather Ledge as in the following route.

Kinloss Corner   120m   VI,6**
A. Paul & D. Sanderson   January 1984
A short, technical and sustained route which starts 15m left of and below North Face Route where a slab leads to a corner. Climb the slab and corner and a second easier slab leading to a short open corner. Climb the corner then a rib on the left of another corner which leads to an easier ledge (Heather Ledge). It is possible to traverse right on the ledge and either abseil or climb down rightwards to easier ground between Central Buttress and D Gully Buttress.

North Face Route   220m   VI**
J.R. Marshall & J. Stenhouse   January 1958
A sustained and difficult mixed route. Climb a series of steep corners, walls, chimneys and cracks on the right (N.E. edge) side of **Central Buttress**. These lead to an easier angled ledge (Heather Ledge). A large white scar may be seen on the North Face above, with a recess beneath it. Gain the recess by traversing round two pillars. Continue the traverse rightwards, descending to a ledge. Climb an awkward 3 metre wall to a right-slanting ledge which is followed to a 20 metre chimney. Climb the chimney to gain a platform then traverse left to short steep crack near the N.E. edge. Follow the edge to the top. Traverse rightwards across the top of D Gully onto Curved Ridge.

Special K   85m   IV*
R. Anderson & A. Russel   21st January 1984
Starts higher up the open easy gully from which Alpen starts and climbs the obvious icefall to the right of a prominent fin of rock at the top of the

BUACHAILLE ETIVE MOR SOUTH EAST FACE (OVERLOOKING GLEN ETIVE)

1. THE CHASM
2. CHASM TO CROWBERRY TOWER TRAVERSE
3. LADY'S GULLY (LEFT FORK)
4. WATERSLIDE GULLY
5. THE VEIL
6. NORTH FACE ROUTE
7. ALPEN
8. SPECIAL K
9. CURVED RIDGE

205

gully. Climb the icefall with difficulty to a belay (40m). Climb the same line, slightly left and trending left to the top of Central Buttress (45m).

Alpen   245m   IV**
S. Belk, I. Fulton, K.V. Crocket, C. Stead   March 1972
Follows the chimneys and small gullies as mentioned below to the left of D Gully Buttress. Start halfway up an easy gully which trends left between D Gully Buttress and Central Buttress, at the foot of a wall. Climb steep turf ledges to the foot of a corner (45m). Continue up the corner to a cave belay (20m). Climb the right wall of the cave (10m), then a chimney and trend more easily left to a small spike belay (40m). Traverse left and belay below the right hand of two parallel chimneys (15m). Climb this chimney and right-ward ramp to a belay (40m). Move up left in the gully (40m) and finish up right to the buttress top (45m).

Left of D Gully Buttress is **Central Buttress,** the two are separated by a wide open bay, from the back of which springs a line of chimneys and small gullies. An approach towards **Central Buttress** can be made by continuing horizontally on a faint track for a further 500m from the **Waterslide Slab** mentioned in the approach to the Crowberry Basin. This approach will put the climber below the rocks of Central Buttress. It is also advisable to drive down Glen Etive for a mile or so in order to sort out the various routes on this complicated face. If a descent into Glen Etive is envisaged, the approach from Glen Etive is in fact shorter.

STOB DEARG - North East Face - Lagangarbh appproach

D Gully Buttress   150m   III
The buttress is narrow and defined by the deep D Gully on the right and on the left by indefinite rocks merging with Central Buttress with which it forms a right-angle. The start of the buttress is vague and entry is usually made from the foot of D Gully. A prominent steep smooth step high up the buttress is a useful landmark. The first section is fairly easy but then the way is blocked by the steep smooth step. Turn on the left by a shallow chimney and gully leading back rightwards to regain the crest, very narrow at this point. Above, a long slabby section gives the crux, usually climbed near its right edge. After a further 30m or so the buttress ends on a shoulder whence a right traverse should be made to gain Curved Ridge and Easy Gully.

D Gully 150m II
G.T. Glover and Collinson April 1898
The gully below and to the left of Curved Ridge. Usually easy but can give several short pitches. At the top traverse up and right to Curved Ridge.

Curved Ridge/Easy Gully 300m II*** (but can attain Grade III after heavy snowfall)
G.T. Glover and R.G. Napier April 1898
A magnificent route to the summit of the mountain, it passes through grand rock scenery, is a good general view point and gives interesting climbing under almost any conditions. Certainly the most useful winter climb on the Buachaille and can be quite hard. The line follows the crest of the ridge throughout. Easier options are available in the gully to the right of the crest (beware of avalanches).

Climb slightly left out of the Crowberry Basin by any of the several variations and pass beneath the Rannoch Wall of Crowberry Ridge (two short steep pitches) to reach a final big cairn, at the top of Curved Ridge proper and below the foot of Crowberry Tower. From the cairn a horizontal left traverse for about 30m brings one onto a snow slope with two gully exits.

1. The gully slanting back to the right reaches the Crowberry Tower Gap and from there a short groove leads left then right to the top of Crowberry Gully and the final summit slopes.

2. The gully going up slightly leftward leads directly to the summit rocks. It is probably the quickest but not the most interesting way.

If time permits, an ascent of the Crowberry Tower can be included if the first route is followed; from the gap a short corner is climbed to a ledge on the left then an easy rising spiral traverse leads to the top. There are more interesting routes up the Tower but this is the easiest and best in descent.

Crowberry Ridge (Naismith's Original Route) 200m III**
From the narrows at the foot of Crowberry Gully proper move up onto the obvious Pinnacle Ledge at the foot of three chimneys. The left-hand chimney is followed.

Climb up to the right and as soon as possible take the easiest line back left to the crest. Continue up the crest with easing difficulty to the Crowberry Tower.

Shelf Route   170m   IV**
W.M. MacKenzie and W.H. Murray   March 1937
A superb and sustained climb if good conditions are present. A shallow
chimney line running up the left wall of Crowberry Gully. Start low
down in Crowberry Gully and traverse left to foot of three chimneys.
Climb the right wall and rib of the middle chimney to a shallow trough
above. Follow the scoop above between the steep left wall and a small
pinnacle. Possible escapes over iced slabs to the ridge on the left. The
direct line continues to a recess under the pinnacle from where an
awkward right traverse is made to gain icy grooves which lead up to the
ridge below Crowberry Tower. Either climb the tower direct and
descend its right side to the col (Crowberry Gap) or traverse left towards
the top of Curved Ridge.

Crowberry Gully   300m   III/IV***
H. Raeburn, W.A. Brigg and H.S. Tucker   April 1909
A magnificent classic climb of considerably quality. Unfortunately it is
not often in good condition and can be dangerous due to avalanches.
Conditions vary remarkably and can change in a short space of time. It
may be completely banked up with snow except for an ice pitch at the
junction (where a rightwards rising traverse is made from the foot of the
deep recessed Left Fork) and another pitch at the exit from a cave near
the top of the gully. The cave will usually give the crux of the normal
route (although the Junction pitch can also be quite hard) climbed by the
right wall which is invariably of green ice and 10/15m in height. If
attempted when out of condition (particularly early in the season) there
could be many more pitches and Junction and Cave pitches may be all
but impossible with only a thin veneer of verglas.

Crowberry Gully, Left Fork   IV
R.J. Taunton and I.C. Robertson   18th March 1949
The Left Fork leads steeply out of the main gully to Crowberry Tower
Gap. The deeply recessed gully soon becomes a narrow iced chimney
which is capped by a large overhanging block. The capstone will always
be difficult but good protection is available. Although it is a hard
technical problem, this fork is very short and shouldn't require as much
time as a complete ascent by the normal route. (Rarely climbed.) On the
first ascent, a third member of the party could not be pulled over the
capstone after the second man had stood on his head to gain elevation!!

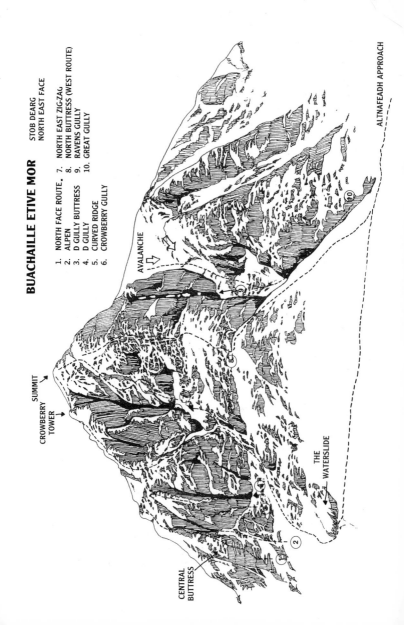

BUACHAILLE ETIVE MOR STOB DEARG
NORTH EAST FACE

1. NORTH FACE ROUTE,
2. ALPEN
3. D GULLY BUTTRESS
4. D GULLY
5. CURVED RIDGE
6. CROWBERRY GULLY
7. NORTH EAST ZIG-ZAG
8. NORTH BUTTRESS (WEST ROUTE)
9. RAVENS GULLY
10. GREAT GULLY

ALTNAFEADH APPROACH

AVALANCHE

SUMMIT

CROWBERRY TOWER

CENTRAL BUTTRESS

THE WATERSLIDE

North East Zig-Zag   100m   III*
J.R. Marshall, A.H. Hendry and G.J. Ritchie   1957
An interesting climb in open surroundings which has many variations
and is clear of the avalanche problems in Crowberry Gully. Start from
the left end of a broad terrace above and right of Crowberry Gully. Move
up left and then back right by the simplest line to gain the upper section
of North Buttress.

North Buttress (West Route) 300m   III***
First winter ascent not recorded but for an account of an early ascent of
the route (and several others in this guide) see *Mountaineering in
Scotland* by W.H. Murray. This is the huge buttress to the left of Great
Gully, and right of Crowberry Gully. From the foot of Great Gully two
alternatives are possible, the first aims straight up easy ground for the
line of chimneys splitting the middle section of the buttress. After 130m
these lead onto easier angled slopes with the odd difficult step. An
easier approach is to continue along the path past the Water Slide and
climb the lower reaches of Crowberry Gully to the Basin. From here
traverse rightwards to join the chimneys of the first approach.

Slime Wall is the very steep rocky cliff left of Raven's Gully and
overlooking Great Gully.

Misty High   195m   V,5**
A. Paul and D. Sanderson   17th March 1979
This climb follows an icefall on the extreme left side of Slime Wall. Up
the icefall and follow the right-hand chimney. Climb easier ground to
a short chimney and under a chockstone to North Buttress. Follow
icefall on the right for two long pitches to easier ground.

Guerdon Grooves   180m   IX,8
D. Cuthbertson and A. Paul   28th January 1984
Technical and very serious with poorly protected leads on steep rock
and ice. The belays are satisfactory! The obvious icy grooves to the left
of Raven's Gully are followed for three pitches into Raven's Gully. From
the flake belay in Raven's Gully the left-hand finish is taken.

Raven's Gully   135m   V,6**
H. MacInnes and C. Bonington   14th February 1953

The dark slit high up on the North Buttress (left) wall of Great Gully. When in condition (fairly often) the crux is soon reached, a large chockstone. Above three or four long difficult pitches lead to the top. A popular classic. The Direct Finish is rarely in condition.

A descent into Great Gully can be made after finishing Raven's Gully. This is only advised if avalanche potential is low and daylight is available to find a route down.

Raven's Edge   140m   VI,7***
S. Allen and B. Sprunt   24th January 1984
Start at the Foot of Raven's Gully. Climb the left edge of the buttress to a large block 10m above the chockstone in Raven's Gully (30m). Climb the vertical wall above then traverse left to a prominent corner which is followed to a ledge (25m). Climb a rib on the right of the corner to a platform (25m). Climb up to a belay below the big roof on the extreme left edge of the buttress (30m). Traverse left under the roof to a very exposed place on the right wall of Raven's Gully and climb a deep crack to the top (30m).

The Long Chimney   135m   V,6**
R. Smith and D. Leaver   15th December 1957
Follow the Ordinary Route to the broad terrace then traverse hard right and climb the long obvious shallow chimney.

Ordinary Route   135m   V,6**
J.R. Marshall, D.N. Mill and G.J. Ritchie   15th December 1957
Start at the lowest rocks near the foot of Raven's Gully and climb to a broad terrace. From its right end climb a short steep pitch followed by grooves to another broad ledge beneath the vertical upper section of the cliff. Traverse right around an exposed edge onto the west face. Climb an obvious shelf then turn towards the centre of the cliff which is climbed to the top.

Cuneiform Corner   60m   IV
A. Paul and D. Sanderson   17th March 1979
To the right of Raven's Gully is a large buttress (Cuneiform Buttress) which overlooks Great Gully. Mid-way up this buttress an obvious icefall/corner is followed in two pitches to a terrace from where a traverse right into Great Gully can be made.

N.B. It is possible to continue to the summit by following steep corners/ grooves and icy walls above the traverse line for another 170m *(P. Moores and C. Butler February 1983 Grade III).*

Great Gully   360m   I/II*
Norman Collie   1894
The first deep gully to cross the path about 20 minutes from Lagan-garbh. It is sometimes confused with easier gullies further west. Early in the season it can give several hundred feet of ice, but generally banks out with frequent and considerable avalanche danger.

THE AONACH EAGACH RIDGE

The Aonach Eagach is the long notched ridge which bounds Glen Coe to the north applying particularly to the narrow crest extending between Sgor nam Fionnaidh on the west to Am Bodach at the east end. The Glen Coe flank of this ridge is steep and complex, very rocky and seamed by many gullies.

The Aonach Eagach Traverse   3kms to end   II/III***
In good weather and good conditions the ridge gives a very fine winter expedition. Speed is essential if the party is to avoid an all too frequent benightment. The normal route is from east to west which gives one the advantage of 100m less to climb. Best starting point is from near the white cottage at Allt-na-Reigh. Parking available just down the road (GR 173567). A track leads up, crossing the stream, into the corrie to the east of Am Bodach whence easy slopes lead leftwards to the top (943m). Alternatively one may continue directly up the ridge from the start. Not advised in descent.

The descent from Am Bodach to the west can be quite difficult: go slightly right then back left and down a gully-crack. The most interesting section of the ridge is between Meall Dearg (953m) and Stob Coire Leith (940m), particularly a very narrow pinnacled section and an awkward slabby descent beyond it.

It must be pointed out that there is no safe descent from the ridge on the Glen Coe flank between the two end peaks. It is best to continue to the end of the ridge and descend from Sgor nam Fionnaidh to the saddle between it and the Pap of Glen Coe. With care it may be possible to descend towards Loch Leven in a northerly direction at a number of points along the ridge.

OUTLYING CLIMBS IN GLEN COE

A'CHAILLACH S.E. FACE
Red Funnel Gully   200m   I/II
R. Baillie, H. MacInnes and party   1964
Interesting for an easy day after heavy snow. It overlooks the road through the gorge at the top of the Glen on the Aonach Eagach side and follows the left fork of the steepest gully.

GLEN ETIVE
Dalness Chasm   400m   IV***
H. MacInnes and C. Williamson   February 1979
This obvious watercourse lies opposite the first cottage down Glen Etive, some 6¹/₂kms from the main road. A tremendous climb, though rarely in condition. Follow the main stream line with one big pitch until the triple fork is reached. Take the right fork by steep, short pitches.
Central Fork (VI,5)   **Left Fork** (VI,5)

BEINN TRILLEACHAN - ETIVE SLABS
(GS 0944 - Sheet 50 - 1:50,000 O.S. Map)
After several days of hard frost, water smears running down the slabs begin to freeze. Two climbs have been made. The first follows an ice smear near the right side of the main slabs and then tackles roofs and mixed ground above. The second Dan, Grade IV, takes a much thicker line of ice up the subsidiary buttress just up and to the right of the main slabs. Worth a look for a short day.

SRON NA LAIRIG   300m   I/II*
A prominent rocky spur overlooking the head of Lairig Eilde and leading up onto the south-east ridge of Stob Coire Sgreamhach. The approach up the Larig is quite long but gentle. The lower part is best avoided on the left, but higher up it narrows to a fine crest. A good primer for the Aonach Eagach.

SGOR NA H-ULAIDH 994m (GR 111518)
This fine but remote peak lies to the west of Bidean and has several easy

climbs on the north face of the mountain. The conspicuous, deep gully directly below the summit gives three or four good pitches and is called Red Gully - Grade III.

N.B. This is a difficult mountain to descend from in poor visibility.

STOB A'GHLAIS CHOIRE 996m   (GR 240516)

Well seen from the Kingshouse the N.E. Face of this mountain appears to be seamed with steep gullies and ridges. On closer inspection the angle relents. However, the routes are all worthwhile for climbers searching for easier ascents away from the crowds. Access is governed by the amount of water in the River Etive. When the river is low it is possible to cross at a number of spots, either before or after Coupall Bridge (GR 243543) and skirt the foot of Creag Dhubh. Allow 1¹/₂ hours for either approach. In descent the corrie S.E. of the summit of Stob a'Ghlais Choire can be taken. Care should be exercised on these slopes after strong winds or snowfalls, as wind slab avalanches may be present. A longer but more satisfying end to a climb would involve ascending both Creise, 1,110m (GR 238507) and Meall a'Bhuiridh, 1,108m (GR 251503). A descent could then be made through the ski area to the north.

The nature of all the gullies will vary depending on the amount of snow build-up. They will all be easy, Grade I or II. The ridges which separate the gullies are worthy of inspection and will provide steeper mixed climbing at Grade II/III. Also the right-hand skyline will provide an interesting route of ascent, with more difficulty nearer the top. Of particular interest to the climber is the following route:

Inglis Clark Ridge   140m   III*
R. Napier and S. Downie   March 1987
In the centre of the N.E. Face is a broad V-shaped buttress just left of No.5 Gully, the top of which is a flat-topped tower. Start at the right-hand end of the ridge, 30m up No.5 Gully. Follow grooves and some steep ice pitches (crux) to a broad terrace (35m). Ascend to the rock tower and climb it on the right to a wall (65m). Traverse left (5m) along the wall and then up right by blocks and a right-angled corner chimney to the top of the tower.

STOB A'GHLAIS CHOIRE

1. GULLY 1
2. GULLY 2
3. GULLY 3
4. GULLY 4
5. INGLIS CLARK RIDGE
6. GULLY 5
7. NAPIER'S BUTTRESS
8. GULLY 6
9. GULLY 7

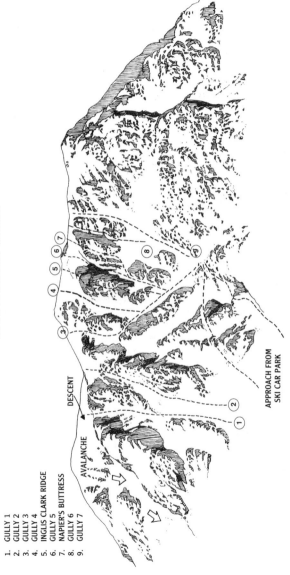

DESCENT

AVALANCHE

APPROACH FROM
SKI CAR PARK

215

Original grades are shown in the index for historical reference only.
New grades (for harder) routes appear in text.

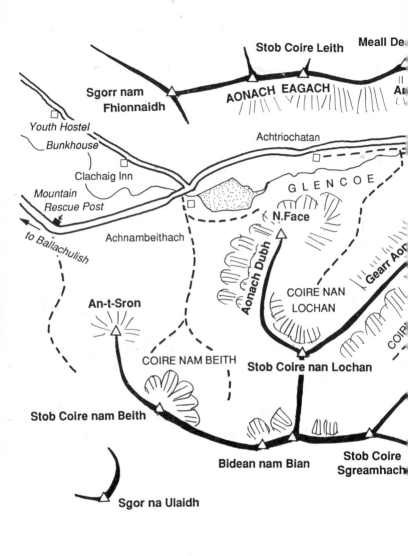